ACPL, Laramie, WY   08/20 17
000400884642
Kaniut, Larry.
Cheating death : amazing s
Pieces: 1

D0349638

**ALBANY COUNTY
PUBLIC LIBRARY**
Serving the Laramie Plains since 1887

Laramie, Wyoming 82070

PRESENTED BY

A Friend

CHEATING
DEATH

Amazing Survival Stories
from Alaska

CHEATING DEATH

Amazing Survival Stories from Alaska

Larry Kaniut

Illustrations by Brian Sostrom

Epicenter Press

Fairbanks/Seattle

ALBANY COUNTY
PUBLIC LIBRARY
LARAMIE, WYOMING

Editor: Don Graydon, Kent Sturgis
Proofreader: Christine Ummel
Illustrations, maps: Brian Sostrom
Jacket design: Elizabeth Watson
Design and pre-press production: Laing Communications Inc.
Printing/binding supervised by Ripinsky & Co. Production Services
Text © 1994 Larry Kaniut

This is an Earth-friendly book printed on recycled, acid-free paper.

All rights reserved. No part of this publication may be reproduced, stored in a retrieval system, or transmitted, in any form or by any means, electronic, mechanical, photocopying, recording, or otherwise without the prior written permission of the publisher. Permission is given for brief excerpts to be published with book reviews in newspapers, magazines, newsletters and catalogs.

Library of Congress Cataloging-in-Publication Data

Kaniut, Larry.
    Cheating death: amazing survival stories from Alaska / by Larry
Kaniut: illustrations by Brian Sostrom.
        p.   cm.
    ISBN 0-945397-23-2: $19.95
    1. Wilderness survival—Alaska. I. Title.
GV200.5.K36 1994
613.6'7—dc20   94-2798
                                                                              CIP

To order single, autographed copies of CHEATING DEATH, mail $19.95 (Washington residents add $1.64 sales tax) plus $5 for priority-mail shipping to: Epicenter Press, Box 82368, Kenmore Station, Seattle, WA 98028-0368.

Booksellers: Retail discounts are available from our trade distributor, Graphic Arts Center Publishing Co., Box 10306, Portland, OR 97210. Phone 800-452-3032.

PRINTED IN THE UNITED STATES OF AMERICA

First printing, April 1994

10 9 8 7 6 5 4 3 2 1

To the brave individuals whose stories fill these pages.

And in memory of Ray Flickinger,

my high school Brother of the Fire Ring.

Some say God was tired when he made it;
Some say it's a fine land to shun;
Maybe; but there's some as would trade it
For no land on earth — and I'm one.

—Robert Service, *The Spell of the Yukon*

Contents

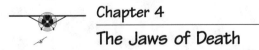

A glacier dam of snow and ice bursts, sending a surge of water into the Copper River. The life of Kevin Smith is forever changed as his raft collides with the river's swollen rapids.

In a freak accident, Jim Aronow is dragged beneath the sea by a plummeting anchor. If he can find his knife, he may be able to cut through the line that holds him in a death grip.

Acknowledgments

With a deep sense of appreciation, I want to thank the people whose remarkable stories are told in this book. Their selfless sharing of difficult experiences is a great gift to those of us who can learn from their confrontations with disaster.

I also owe thanks to the many friends who continue to alert me to new stories of people who have faced tragedy in the outdoors and managed to cheat death.

Many thanks to my editor, Don Graydon, and my publisher, Kent Sturgis, for their fine work in bringing this collection of stories to publication.

I appreciate the support of my children — Ginger, Jill, and Ben — whose lives are a constant inspiration to me.

I give great thanks to Pam — my wife and loyal adviser-editor — for her countless hours of work on my manuscripts and for her encouragement.

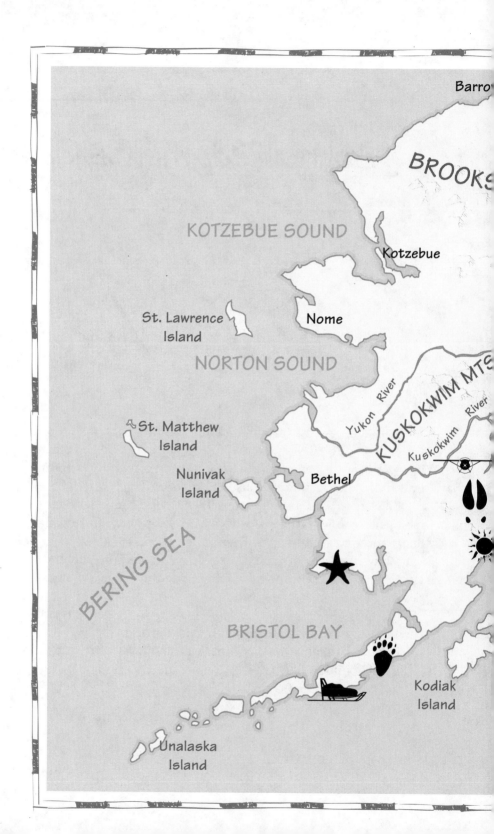

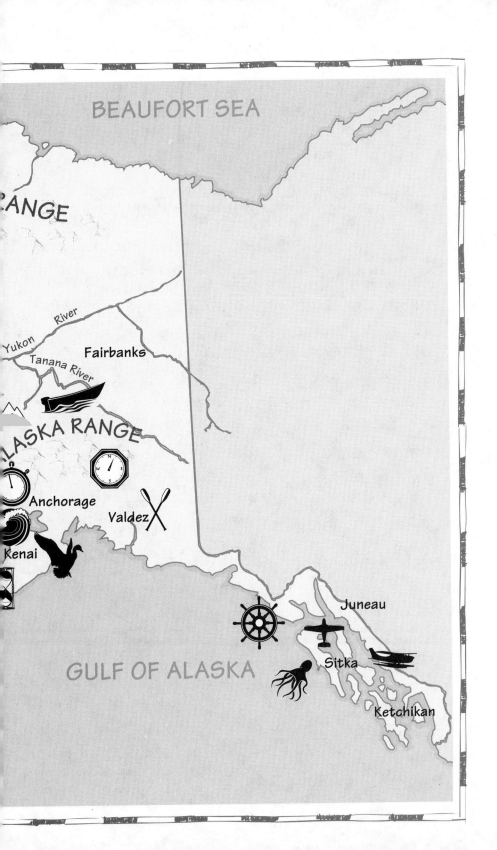

Introduction

Living with Danger

As beautiful as nature is, one has to always respect it. It seldom gives a second chance.

—James Marchini,
writing in *Alaska* magazine

Whether or not you're a veteran of your own heart-pounding adventure in the outdoors, try to imagine yourself clinging for life to a tiny iceberg as it sweeps you down a frigid Alaska river. Or picture yourself struggling to fight your way out of a submerged airplane. Or digging out of a frozen grave as avalanche after avalanche engulfs you. Or returning to consciousness in a wilderness snowstorm, your airplane scattered in pieces around you. Or battling impossible odds to jockey a jet boat up an unrunnable river.

Some people did not imagine these experiences; they lived them. These true stories and many more fill this book. They are not embellished. They are the stories of people who ventured into the Alaskan outdoors and returned, just barely, to tell about it.

Alaska is a great state for survival stories. Although other states encompass wilderness in which their citizens confront peril, no state can match danger on an Alaskan scale. Alaska is twice as big as Texas. Alaska's coastline is as long as that of the rest of the United States. Alaska's topography is more extreme than that of the other states. Her mountains are bigger. Her rivers are colder. Her weather is harsher. Her lakes are unnumbered, and much of her vastness is untracked.

Because Alaskans are surrounded by untamed wilderness, outdoors hardship and tragedy are not unusual. The lights of the city don't guarantee safety, because danger lies just beyond the doorstep. A review of newspaper articles for only a single week in summer revealed a spate of Alaskan-style accidents:

Biologist suffers hypothermia and broken bones in 1,300-foot fall . . . Soldier survives mauling from grizzly sow with cubs . . . Airplane hits cliff, killing six summer employees from Glacier Bay National Park . . . Teen twins killed by ledge of ice near Point Hope while ivory fossil hunting . . . Lost hunter's body found . . . Bear attacks woman on Juneau street . . . Four men die in Ketchikan plane crash.

Part of the lure of Alaska is the chance to live on the Last Frontier — to experience the rugged beauty, high adventure, and challenge it offers. Most who go afield return unharmed, but some do not. And that's the risk of venturing into Alaska's bush.

Some of the heroes of this book were newcomers to Alaska; others were old hands at dealing with its demands. But novice or veteran, all confronted a moment that found them at the thin edge between survival and tragedy. We can usually point to the factors that brought them to that edge. As you read these tales, look for recurring themes: bad weather, treacherous terrain, mechanical failure, poor preparation, ignorance, bad judgment, overconfidence.

Alaska is a land of such wonder that we sometimes drift into the dangerous habit of looking on the uncommon as common — forgetting that the power of current or tide is mindless, that the snout of the glacier spins off huge blocks of ice, that mud flats suck the unsuspecting into their clutches. Many of us are guilty of letting our supposed mastery of the wilderness lull us into the sleep of improper preparation. Often it is mere fractions — in distance, time, or preparation — that make the difference between life and death.

Preparation, common sense, and caution are insulators against disaster, but they're no guarantee of safety. To enter the wilderness, you need proper knowledge and adequate gear. You need to honestly know your own limitations. You need a partner, preferably one with bush experience. And finally, when you face your own moment at the edge, you need the will to live. Classic stories of survival send a simple but resounding message: don't give up hope — ever. When you lose that hope and that will to live, you die. ■

We broke free of the mud and swam to the ice.

1

In the Knik of Time

I kicked the door open. We tumbled from the plane. A wall of water smashed us off our feet and rolled over our heads. The frigid water was paralyzing.

 Marvin Milam got on the radio to Anchorage's Merrill Field. "We're five miles north, altitude six hundred feet. We're going down in the inlet. Need help." Thus began the fight of Milam and his passenger to survive a wintery forced landing in Knik Arm at the upper end of Cook Inlet as one of the highest tides on earth rose quickly around them. Passenger Ken Broussard tells the story.

MARVIN MILAM, A SURVEYOR, was thirty-six years old, four years older than I. We worked for N.L. Sperry Sun Company, an oil-related firm, in Anchorage. On the morning of March 5, 1981, Marvin asked me if I'd like to join him in his Cessna 180 for a flight to Big Lake for lunch. I'd never been in a small plane; I thought it sounded great. So we drove out to Merrill Field.

I was ready to jump into the airplane when I got my first surprise. Marvin handed me an ice chipper, the kind you use to scrape your car windshield. "You start on the left," he said, "and I'll start on the right." It took us well over an hour to scrape off every bit of the thin layer of ice that covered the metal-skinned plane.

My next surprise came when we landed on ice-covered Big Lake after a ten-minute flight. I'd never heard of landing a plane this way. A road had been plowed through the snow on top of the frozen lake. We taxied right to Big Lake Lodge.

After a great lunch we hopped into the plane and headed back to Anchorage. On the horizon to the east lay the Chugach Mountains. Between us and Anchorage was Elmendorf Air Force Base. Marvin asked if I'd like a better look at Cook Inlet. I said, "Sure."

We dropped down to six hundred feet. The tide was out, and the mud flats looked cold and bare. Farther down the inlet, hundreds of gravel-colored chunks of ice the size of small school buses bobbed on the slate-gray surface like giant corks.

Then came the biggest surprise of all. The engine began coughing, *kachooka chooka*. Marvin said the plane was losing power, and he started looking for a landing spot. Then he got on the radio to Merrill Field.

We were about to make a forced landing. Marvin did an excellent job of getting us out of the air. He touched the plane down, and we bounced a couple of times. The nose pitched down, then popped back up. We stopped abruptly. We were shaken up but not hurt.

We had landed on a high point of sand, half a mile from the beach. It was the only high spot in sight. Water surrounded us.

Marvin was having trouble getting through to Merrill Field on the radio. He tried to communicate with the tower at Anchorage International Airport, but no luck. The pilot of a small plane picked up the call and relayed it to Anchorage. The tower gave the pilot a radio frequency for us to use, and the pilot relayed that information down to us.

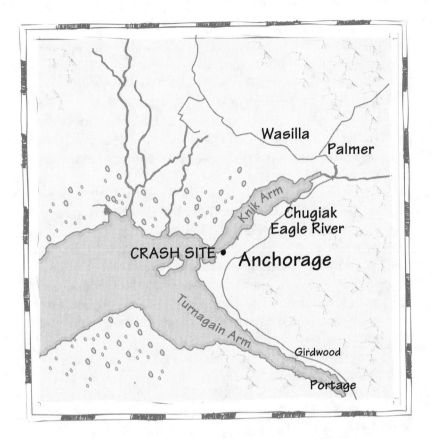

Marvin was talking with the Anchorage controller when we heard a disturbing noise outside the plane. We looked out to see the tide rushing in. Water began pouring through the door.

Marvin immediately signed off with the controller. He knew we were in trouble.

MARVIN DIRECTED ME TO PUT ON ONE of the two Arctic parkas that were in the plane and to give him the other one. He grabbed a couple of items that I didn't recognize, stuffing one into my pocket and the other into his own pocket. "Emergency locator transmitters," he said. "They'll tell searchers where we are." Then he told me to get out of the plane.

Before following me out, Marvin ripped his expensive King radio from its mounts and brought it along. He had installed the radio only a week earlier. I didn't know what faced us, but I was optimistic that within a few minutes we would hear the welcome sound of a helicopter.

I kicked the door open. We tumbled from the plane. A wall of water smashed us off our feet and rolled over our heads. The frigid water was paralyzing; it took my breath away. It was so cold it stung.

I surfaced and struggled to my feet. "Marv!" I yelled for my friend. I gasped for air. Marvin emerged from the other side of the plane. We slogged twenty yards from the plane in the swirling gray water. I had heard that few men live longer than fifteen minutes in this glacier-fed water, with winter temperatures hovering at twenty-eight degrees.

At this point the water was only knee deep, but the tide was barreling in. I was dodging chunks of ice. Quickly the water rose to our waists; suddenly water was halfway up the plane fuselage.

Then Marvin threw his treasured King radio into the water, and I knew we were in trouble a lot worse than I had first thought.

Suddenly we faced a new peril—quicksand. Marvin sank into the gooey muck beneath the surface. It grabbed his boots like a hungry animal. He shouted a warning. He managed to free himself, but lost a boot to the suction of the mud.

A chunk of ice three feet square was floating about thirty feet from us. Marvin figured we could ride it. We broke free of the mud and swam to the ice. He told me to reach across the ice and grab hold of his collar. He did the same thing, supporting his arms on the block of ice and holding tight to my parka collar.

I looked to my right, at the shoreline. I'd swum all my life in Louisiana. "Marvin, let go of me," I said. "I'm going to swim to the bank."

"You'll never make it," he said. "Don't even think about it." Marvin, who is six-foot-three and weighs two-twenty-five, held onto me real tight. Thank God, because thirty seconds later I was numb from my neck down. I couldn't move my legs or anything else. If I had tried to swim away, I would have drowned right in front of Marvin.

The tide was pushing us north toward Palmer at six knots. We talked the whole time, wondering where our rescuers were and how long we could endure the excruciating cold. Other chunks of ice continually banged into us, jarring us violently.

We'd been in the water for thirty minutes. I stared blankly into Marvin's eyes. My earlier belief that everything would be all right had long since left me. Our energy was gone. We had reached our physical limits, and emotionally we were near hopelessness.

My lips were gray. My shoulders and body slumped. Marvin forced himself to shake my collar, but I could not acknowledge his support. I felt lifeless.

Near the end I looked up to my right and saw a large aircraft several hundred feet above our heads.

SHORTLY AFTER MARVIN MILAM and Ken Broussard made their forced landing, an Air Rescue C-130 on a training mission picked up a signal from an emergency locator transmitter. The pilot, Major Frank Mason, radioed Elmendorf Air Force Base's Rescue Coordination Center in Anchorage, 110 miles south of his position near Farewell.

The officer in charge at the center, Major Ned Newman, told Mason that the signal came from a Cessna, with two people aboard, that had been reported down in Cook Inlet. Mason's help was urgently needed. The C-130 Kingbird, flying at 400 miles an hour, could reach the site before an emergency plane and crew could get off the ground in Anchorage. Mason knew he could be over the inlet in minutes. He also knew that might not be soon enough.

Shortly after Mason called the rescue center, a helicopter landed at Elmendorf to refuel. It was immediately ordered aloft. Captain Buster Hampton and his co-pilot, First Lieutenant Larry Sandoval, got the helicopter airborne within minutes. Hampton's crew consisted of flight engineer Bob Hoak and parajumpers Alex Wassuta and Skip Kula, who were trained in water rescue.

Hampton couldn't imagine anyone surviving long in the churning waters below. The inlet's rip tides and currents were notorious in summer; they were even more hazardous now with the accumulation of winter ice and slush. Knik Arm was a frothy cauldron. Crew members strained their eyes for a glimpse of the men below. All they saw was tons of ice, slush, and scattered logs jamming the water.

Aboard the C-130, Major Mason ordered flares dropped to provide visual reference for the chopper pilot. He hoped the helicopter could follow the smoke trail to the source of the emergency locator signals.

WITHIN MINUTES WE HEARD the sound of a helicopter. But then to my despair I saw that the chopper was on the wrong side of the inlet and heading north. Even in my lethargic state, this terrible fact registered. *They're not going to get here in time*, I thought. Then the chopper turned and started coming toward us.

Marvin shook me. I blinked, acknowledging understanding. But my mind was in a fog. I thought, *It's just a matter of time until we're spotted, but can we hold out that long?*

The helicopter spotted us and made three or four circles right above us. And that was the most scared I felt the entire time. Because as the helicopter circled, I began thinking, *Oh, God, this chopper can't pull us out of the water. It's an observation chopper of some kind. He doesn't have the ability to hoist us up.* That really scared me because I could only last a few more minutes. After hanging on for forty minutes, time was about up. I didn't think I was going to make it.

ON BOARD THE CHOPPER Alex Wassuta donned his rescue gear. Within minutes he was ready, and the doors opened.

The crew knew the downwash of the chopper blades caused a serious problem for the two men below. The combination of the cold and the tremendous force of the blades created frigid air that made the men even colder. And unless the chopper could maintain a hover directly over the men, there was great danger of knocking them off the ice.

Below the chopper Ken and Marvin appeared lifeless, just two heads floating above the surface. It was probably too late. The chopper crew would probably be picking up two dead men.

Alex was lowered on a cable seat until it was safe for him to jump into the water.

WE WERE GETTING BLASTED pretty good from the chopper downdraft. Alex Wassuta swam over to us. He broke me free of Marvin. They lowered a cable with a triple hook on it, and Alex attached me to the hoisting system. He gave a hand signal and up I went. About halfway up I came loose from part of the straps and fell off one hook. But another hook, attached near my chest, held me.

Skip Kula grabbed me and pulled me into the helicopter. He began giving me oxygen and put heating pads under my arms. He stripped my clothes off (my whole body had red streaks on it) and threw me into some kind of sleeping bag. I was shaking uncontrollably.

They hoisted Marvin into the helicopter and laid him next to me. Then I blacked out.

At Providence Hospital in Anchorage, we were given over to Dr. William J. Mills, Jr., an authority on frostbite and hypothermia. I was laid on my back on a device that looked like a big board with chains hooked to a ceiling hoist. They covered me with warm towels.

I was still trembling violently as Dr. Mills began my treatment. I felt this intense pain as he inserted a catheter into my penis. Then they attached two intravenous tubes to my arms. They were simultaneously pumping fluids into and out of me. I was later told that body core temperature in a state of coma is eighty-nine degrees, and I was down to ninety. My legs were at seventy-five degrees.

They lowered me into and out of a warm bath solution. Each time they lowered me into the bath, I could feel the water getting a little warmer. But I kept shaking violently.

Marvin told me later that when he was brought into the hospital, he took one look at me and thought, "Man, Broussard must be bad off. Look what they're doing." Two minutes later they were doing the same thing to him.

After our second day in the hospital, Doctor Mills told us that we were the fifty-fourth and fifty-fifth patients he'd treated who had suffered hypothermia from immersion in Cook Inlet. He said we were the first ones to survive the hypothermia.

MARVIN AND I SWEAR TO THIS DAY that while we were in the water, we talked the entire forty-two minutes. There's no way anyone can convince me that I was not communicating with Marvin. But Doctor Mills said that after about twenty-five minutes in those conditions, it's physically impossible for people to speak. It would have been done through mental telepathy. But we swear we talked to each other the whole time.

The main reason I'm here sharing our story is that Marvin talked me through the whole ordeal. "Hold on as tight as you can," he kept insisting. "Everything's gonna be fine. They know where we are."

After we recovered, Marvin and I flew over the inlet at low tide to see if we could find his plane. We couldn't find a bolt. The thirty-foot tides of the inlet had thrashed it into a million pieces.

A year later Marvin built a lodge at Talkeetna and named it Latitude 62. He hung one of the emergency locator transmitters from the ceiling. We have a party every year to celebrate our survival. ∎

It was only a matter of time before the skiff also sank.

2

Madness in the Bay

The ice and rocks striking the water created a giant, churning wave. Bill lunged to the wheelhouse. Their only hope was to start the motor and get the bow turned into the wave. If they could ride the wave, they would have a chance at survival.

 It was the end of the day on July 9, 1958. Bill and Vi Swanson had experienced some of their best salmon fishing in years. After a full day aboard their forty-six-foot commercial troller *Badger*, Bill and Vi anticipated a restful night before another busy day of trolling along the rugged coast of Southeast Alaska. They were approaching Lituya Bay — and an amazing adventure.

GLACIERS AND SEAS gouged out Lituya Bay, which runs directly inland from the Gulf of Alaska for almost eight miles and ends in a T-shaped head a couple of miles long. A geologic fault line hundreds of feet below the surface runs the entire length of the bay's head.

Lituya Glacier, which flows into the north side of the bay's head, lies hidden from the view of anyone out on the main body of the bay. Where the glacier meets the bay, house-sized chunks of ice calve off and drop into the water.

Bill and Vi Swanson were familiar with the checkered history of Lituya Bay. In 1786, French explorer Jean La Perouse witnessed the deaths of twenty-one of his men as they were swept out to sea by a strong ebb tide. The survivors erected a monument to the dead on the island in the center of the bay, which La Perouse named Cenotaph. A tidal wave later swept Cenotaph and destroyed the monument.

Another tidal wave struck in 1853, destroying a Tlingit Indian village. In 1899 a severe earth tremor shook the Lituya Bay region.

On October 27, 1936, trapper-prospector Jim Huscroft was preparing breakfast on Cenotaph Island when he and his partner heard a roar. A fifty-foot wave rumbled down the bay, flooding Huscroft's cabin and claiming fifty barrels of salmon.

Nearby, Fritz Erickson and Nick Larson were aboard the trolling boat *Mine*. The wave raised the boat fifty feet above normal water level — and then bounced the boat off the sea bottom as it subsided. No one knows whether the wave was generated by the breaking of an ice dam or by an earthquake.

ON JULY 9, 1958, the Swansons chugged into Lituya Bay through its narrow entrance, known for its tricky currents. They anchored three-quarters of a mile from the mouth. They had a good view of the mountain to the northeast that blocks any sight of Lituya Glacier. Their friends Orville and Mickey Wagner were anchored only a couple of hundred yards away from them in the *Sunmore*.

The Swansons and the Wagners were unaware that an earthquake had hit earlier in the day near Yakutat, about one hundred miles to the northwest.

For the moment, the Swansons enjoyed the beauty of the bay. It was now 10 p.m., still daylight, peaceful and calm. Though the

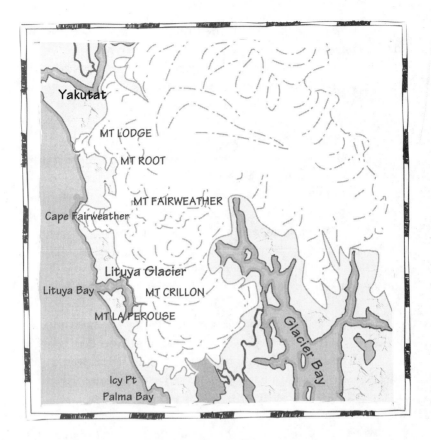

evening was pleasant, an eeriness pervaded the scene. Gradually they realized it resulted from the silence. Cenotaph Island was home to thousands of seagulls, which normally wheeled about the sky in a cacophony of shrieks. But now the birds huddled on the island.

Without warning the birds rose as one, their shrieking calls reverberating across the water. In their haste, some of the gulls hit the *Badger*'s mast and dropped onto her deck.

Bill grabbed Vi's arm and stared toward the head of the bay in stunned awe. The mountain that blocked their view of the glacier suddenly seemed to be belching boulders. In disbelief they watched as the glacier rose above the mountain and with a deafening roar poured countless thousands of tons of ice chunks and rocks into the bay. The earthquake had triggered a massive slide from the glacier.

The ice and rocks striking the water created a giant, churning wave. Bill lunged to the wheelhouse. Their only hope was to start the motor and get the bow turned into the wave. If they could ride the wave, they would have a chance at survival.

The wall of water hit the *Badger*, snapping the anchor loose. The anchor flew upward and embedded itself in the pilothouse. The boat shuddered upward. As Bill fought the wheel, debris rocketed past overhead. Like a floundering hiker climbing upward in deep snow, the *Badger* wallowed its way up the wave.

The *Sunmore* was not so fortunate. It rolled and vanished from view below the frothy surface.

The mammoth wave was crushing the shoreline, ripping centuries-old timber from the shores. In one sweep the thundering wave scoured the foliage from the land and sucked it into the bay. The force of the wave tossed the *Badger* seaward across the entrance to the bay and out into the Gulf of Alaska. There the deadly monster wave disappeared seaward into the night.

BILL'S CONTROL of the boat was complicated by the trees and the blocks of ice that now strangled the water and pounded holes in the hull. The *Badger*'s engine had quit, leaving them dead in the water. The stern was underwater, and they were sinking. Trees and icebergs, carried on whitecaps, hammered the *Badger*.

Bill and Vi held out little hope of rescue. No one knew where they were. Even if another boat was near, rescuers probably wouldn't be able to spot them through the darkening sky. And the churning debris-choked seas would keep rescuers away even if the *Badger* was spotted.

Vi struggled with her fears. She knew her faith would sustain her, and her belief in the Bible's message comforted her. Bill stepped toward the cabin to retrieve her Bible just as a tree smashed into the cabin, slamming Bill into the side of the pilothouse. He was knocked down, clutching his chest. He struggled back to Vi, assured her that he was OK, and gave her the Bible.

Their last hope was the skiff. Bill frantically worked to release the rope securing it. Just as he loosened the rope, a wave jerked the skiff away from him. He jumped for the skiff as Vi simultaneously lost her balance and rolled overboard into the sea. She managed to grab the anchor line and to hang on. Bill maneuvered the skiff over to Vi and pulled her aboard.

The skiff had no oars, so Bill paddled with the thwart, which he'd ripped free. Vi used Bill's shoes for bailing water, which rolled incessantly into the skiff. Every stroke of the thwart brought agony to Bill's chest, and each breath was a knifelike stab. Realizing his efforts were futile against the seas, Bill stopped paddling altogether.

Moments later they heard their troller slip beneath the surface of the sea. They continued to bail, fingers becoming numb. As water poured in, they knew it was only a matter of time before the skiff also sank.

They heard a noise. Could it be a boat's engine? They saw a shaft of light through the darkness. Rescuers? Bill and Vi shouted as the searchlight darted everywhere but on them. The frustration of their situation elicited a plea from Vi, "God, help us."

They heard the sound of the chugging engine as it moved off into the distance, growing fainter and fainter. She heard Bill cry out just before she lost consciousness.

WHILE THE SWANSONS struggled, Julian "Stutz" Graham and his son Ken were patrolling the water, looking for survivors. They didn't think anyone could have survived the wave. Nevertheless they felt compelled to search.

They beamed their searchlight upon the water. Stutz had all but given up when he saw a distant light on land. He decided to make a run toward the light.

As his light's beam crawled across the water, Stutz spotted the Swanson skiff and its occupants. He jockeyed his boat through the clutter and managed to reach the skiff.

Stutz and his son got the Swansons aboard his craft. From there he maneuvered through the litter to open water and motored on to Juneau to get medical help for Bill and Vi.

At the hospital, the Swansons got the treatment they required. When Vi was once again fully conscious, she learned about Stutz Graham and his son saving their lives. And she was told how she had refused to release her grip on her Bible. Her determination to hold onto the Bible seemed to reflect the strength of her faith and to explain how they were able to survive the madness in the bay. ∎

Topsy-turvy, Jim hurtled through the air.

3

Death Played Tag

*They heard, then felt, the next avalanche.
It rushed down the slope, rocketed
across the crevasse, and blasted them
down the hill in their tent.*

 Thirty-three-year-old Jim Sweeney, a carpenter and ski-rescue patrol member from Homer, Alaska, stood five-foot-ten-and-a-half and weighed in at 160 pounds. His thirty-one-year-old climbing partner, engineer Dave Nyman from Anchorage, was powerfully built at five-foot-eight and 175 pounds. Though the climbs they planned to do were difficult, they were up to the task. But nothing they had encountered in their climbing careers could match what they faced over the next two weeks.

J IM SWEENEY WAS A MASTER at climbing the frozen waterfalls of Valdez, Alaska. Nyman had climbed in the Andes, the Alps, the Cascades of the Pacific Northwest, and the Rocky Mountains. Both had climbed in California's Yosemite National Park. Now, like two kids heading to the candy store, Sweeney and Nyman excitedly anticipated their upcoming climbing trip. It was April 14, 1989. They drove to K2 Aviation in Talkeetna, Alaska, and met their pilot, Jim Okonek, who would drop them off in the heart of prime climbing country.

Jim loaded the climbers' skis, sleeping bags, food, tents, and climbing gear into his plane. Blue sky beckoned as they lifted off the runway and turned toward the Ruth Glacier, snuggled deep inside Denali National Park and Preserve in the Alaska Range.

They were soon flying above the floor of the Great Gorge, dwarfed by sheer rock walls. Ruth Glacier, a thirty-five-mile-long river of ice, stretched into the distance like a pearly white field of cotton. Snowcapped spires pierced the sky. Mount McKinley, also known as Denali, stood only twelve miles to the northwest.

In perfect weather, the plane touched down on the glacier at the foot of Mount Dickey and skied to a stop.

The men unloaded their mountain of gear while marveling at the mountains surrounding them. They wanted to climb two nearby peaks, the Moose's Tooth and Mount Johnson. They had their eyes set on the Elevator Shaft route on Mount Johnson, knowing it would be a real test of their skills.

The climbers set up their two-tent base camp in a sheltered area of the glacier. Their climbing gear included body harnesses, several lengths of 165-foot rope, a variety of hardware to use in anchoring themselves to the mountain, the snap-on links known as carabiners, and devices to help them in rappelling (sliding down a rope) and in belaying (holding the rope securely while the other person climbs).

They also had tinted goggles, fiberglass helmets, and the spiked metal plates, crampons, that would attach to their boots for traveling on hard snow and ice. They wore wind-resistant nylon pants and coats over their clothing, including polypropylene thermal underwear.

Jim and Dave spent the weekend climbing nearby, polishing their skills. They tackled Moose's Tooth, but gave up after a day fighting bad rock. They turned their attention to Mount

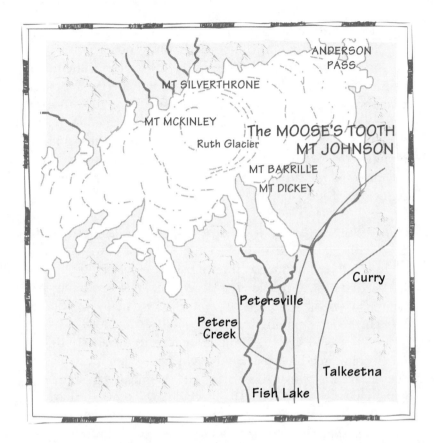

Johnson's demanding Elevator Shaft route, a sheer ice gully (termed a couloir).

First came a one-day scouting trip toward Mount Johnson, checking the Elevator Shaft visually for avalanche danger. Back at base camp, they prepared for an early-morning departure for the climb itself.

Carrying their packs and each pulling a sled with more gear and supplies, they reached the bottom of Mount Johnson the next morning. The first job was to climb the icefall on Johnson's north side. They topped the icefall, more than 600 feet above the base of the wall, and bivouacked for the night.

From the top of the icefall, the plan was to reach the summit via the Elevator Shaft route and return in a single day. They rose early on the morning of April 19 and stashed their sleeping bags and extra gear. They would be traveling light.

They organized their climbing gear and started up the shaft, with Dave in the lead. Using crampons and ice-axe tools, they moved upward, following a methodical system of anchoring, belaying, hauling line in, climbing, resetting anchor pins.

They climbed about 600 feet up the 75-degree incline in less than an hour. Jim was now in the lead. But the ice and snow conditions were deteriorating, the snow becoming rotten — soft and unstable. Finally Jim got a good view of the route ahead. What he saw stunned him. A chasm lay between them and the summit.

Jim could see no safe route. He shouted to his partner, fifty feet below: "Bad going. Maybe we should descend."

THAT'S WHEN THE MOUNTAIN gave way. A huge slab of snow and ice — with Jim aboard — broke loose and shot down the gully. Jim rode it like an immense, thrashing, white bucking bronc. The slab — some thirty feet long, a dozen feet wide and about half that thick — began disintegrating as it fell. Topsy-turvy, Jim hurtled through the air, spinning in the ice chunks and snow.

Instinctively Dave jerked the belay rope to the arrest position so he could catch Jim's fall. He thought he saw Jim rocket past in a blur. Dave was yanked off his feet and slammed against the wall of the gully. Swirling spindrift — windblown snow — filled the air. One of Dave's ice tools popped loose, but his anchor held. When the spindrift settled, a dazed Dave looked down.

Jim's boots stuck out of the snow a hundred feet below. Dave tied off the rope leading to Jim and rappelled down to his pal, expecting the worst. Jim lay motionless, upside down.

Dave clawed the snow and tangled ropes away from Jim, finally cutting the rope with his pocket knife. Jim's helmet was cracked like an eggshell. Blood oozed from his nose and mouth. *He's dead,* Dave thought.

Suddenly Jim tried to talk, his eyes still closed, but it was incoherent babble about the climb. He was apparently oblivious of his spectacular fall.

Then Jim moaned and opened his eyes. Dave was so happy at this positive sign that he kissed Jim. But the situation remained grave. It appeared that Jim's right hip was broken. Dave guessed that he probably also had a skull fracture and possible internal injuries. He had to get him to medical help.

Dave ignored Jim's continued babbling and moved into action. He anchored three ice screws into the face of the gully, clipped

Jim onto the rope, and sat him upright. Jim continued asking Dave what had happened, and insisted that they keep climbing.

Dave knew they had to get out of the line of fire of other avalanches that might come down the chute. Although the combined weight of Jim and his gear equaled his own weight, Dave dragged his partner to a safer spot.

Then Dave climbed back up to the anchor that had held him through Jim's fall. He switched ropes to secure Jim solely to the new anchor and rappelled back down to him. He then began the tedious and exhausting process of lowering Jim, one rope length at a time, down the gully.

It was a long and difficult procedure: Sitting at an anchored position, lower Jim down 165 feet; then tie the end of Jim's rope to the anchor, rappel down to Jim, set new anchor screws, fasten Jim to them, climb back up to the last anchor to untie and retrieve Jim's rope, rappel back down to Jim, lower him another 165 feet, then repeat the process.

Plagued by both falling and blowing snow, Dave took five hours to lower Jim a total of 600 feet. His strength was pushed to the limit. But he was spurred on by Jim's need for medical help and by the dangers of new avalanches and an approaching storm.

Dave finally lowered Jim down off the steepest part of the climb. Then he dug a trench for Jim's protection and elevated his feet to insulate them from the snow. Dave was able to get critical gear and supplies from their old bivouac site: food, down sleeping bags, a stove.

Dave prepared a hot meal and tea. He gave Jim aspirin. Jim's speech became more intelligible. Dave dressed Jim in down clothes before zipping their two bags together, knowing their combined body heat would provide more warmth. Dave had done all he could, and he waited for the dawn.

THEY WERE SHOWERED during the night by small snow slides. As the night progressed, so did the number and size of the slides. Spindrift made breathing difficult. Just before dawn an avalanche blasted the men. Dave dug them out.

While Dave prepared a hot breakfast, Jim asked how the climb was going, renewing Dave fears for Jim's condition.

Dave moved Jim downhill, traversing a couple of hundred feet across a 30-degree slope to a safer spot. Dave gave Jim the last of the aspirin, their last pair of dry socks, and a bottle of water. He got him inside a weatherproof bag and provided an insulation barrier with his own wet sleeping bag.

Dave felt their only hope lay in his skiing to the mountain house seven miles up Ruth Glacier. They talked it over. Jim was afraid Dave would fall into a crevasse. This was quite likely for a person skiing the glacier alone. And Jim was afraid that more avalanches would strike.

Dave had no choice. Without a radio, they could not call for help. He had to chance solo travel on the glacier.

During the morning, he stamped SOS in the snow at two different sites, including their old base camp. He penned a message on some athletic tape and left it at the camp: "Severely injured climber. Location: on north side of Mount Johnson. Helicopter evacuation with medic recommended. Am skiing to Ruth Mountain House for help."

Then he skied off. More than once he crossed a section of snow only to have it drop from sight into a crevasse just after his passing. He reached the mountain house in three and a half hours.

At the house, four skiers were enjoying a four-day vacation. They were reclining on lawn chairs in the sunshine outside the house when they spotted the lone skier coming toward them. They knew something was wrong; no one skis a glacier alone.

Two of the skiers went out to meet Dave, who panted out his story. Dave asked if they had a radio at the house. They didn't. One of the skiers was experienced in mountain rescue and volunteered to take a sleeping bag, candy bars, fuel, aspirin, and a backpack and go with one of the other skiers to Jim's aid. Dave would grab a few hours of badly needed sleep. Assuming Jim would be cared for, Dave crashed into bed.

The two rescuers skied for six hours and found the base camp. But they decided they didn't have the climbing gear they needed to reach Jim. And they feared being caught in an avalanche.

Meanwhile, Jim spent the night alone. Delirious with fever, he tossed and turned and shouted and held conversations with people. He also experienced severe headaches.

Dave awoke at dawn on the 21st, scurried from bed, and struck out down the glacier to find Jim. The remaining two vacationing skiers accompanied him a short distance and then returned to the mountain house. He pressed on alone.

Rounding a corner, Dave was shocked to see the two volunteers who had gone to rescue Jim. Dave's immediate thought was that Jim was dead. But when he reached them, they revealed that they had turned back because of the danger. Disgusted at this news, and fearful again for Jim, Dave was more determined than ever to save his friend. The skiers decided not to accompany Dave, so he carried on alone.

Safely negotiating the glacier a second time, Dave reached base camp, where he added a tent, down bag, liter of stove fuel, and six days' food to his load. He left a new note asking for help.

A cacophony of sounds met Dave as he approached Jim's spot. Avalanches were exploding off the mountains. Dave heard his friend's urgent shout: "I'm being buried." An avalanche had just swept Jim several yards down the mountain, burying him in snow up to his chest.

Dave reached Jim, freed him, and got him into dry clothes and a dry sleeping bag. He dragged Jim a couple of hundred feet and maneuvered him into the tent. Temperatures hovered in the twenties.

Dave set up a new camp behind a ten-by-twenty-foot block of ice, hoping the block would split any avalanches into two streams, which would then flow safely past the tent. He gave Jim aspirin and prepared a hot meal and tea.

The next day, Dave moved the tent, but the new site appeared to be no improvement. Another avalanche hit, knocking the gear from their tent and partially burying it. Mother Nature seemed to be playing cat and mouse with the climbers.

IN A ROUNDABOUT WAY, a rescue scenario now began developing. Pilot Mark Niver was making a flightseeing tour of Ruth Glacier from Big Lake. His passengers were his pregnant wife, Roberta, and a friend, Marie Dunkel.

As the plane flew over the mountain house, Niver saw the word HELP in the snow below. Weather conditions weren't conducive to landing, and his thirteen years of Alaskan flying told him that setting down would be dangerous. But he couldn't ignore the plea for help. He reduced power on his Super Cub, set the wing flaps, and settled down toward the snow. At the last moment he tried to abort the landing, but he stalled the plane and it flopped down hard onto the glacier.

No one was injured, but the plane would not be able to take off. The plane's radio proved useless when Niver tried to call out. However, the emergency locator transmitter began sending signals, which were picked up by the Rescue Coordination Center at Elmendorf Air Force Base in Anchorage and passed on to the National Park Service at Talkeetna.

Later, Niver was able to get out a radio message telling of the injured climber on Mount Johnson. Bob Siebert of the National Park Service's Talkeetna ranger station contacted several climbers who knew Mount Johnson to get information about the peak. The weather was not cooperating; Ruth Glacier was socked in.

DAVE AND JIM rested snugly in their tent despite falling temperatures and heavy snow. They tried to relax, but they knew that most avalanches occur in just such heavy snowfall conditions. Before long the valley resounded with the roars of cascading snow and ice as avalanches rumbled down mountains.

The wind picked up to seventy-five miles per hour and hammered their tent. Dave strained to hold the aluminum stakes in place while reciting the Lord's Prayer. A fear he'd never known possessed him. He knew no one could reach them in such weather.

The storm raged all night and into the next day. That morning their tent was buried, and Dave dug them out. Each avalanche stole away some of their equipment. The tent poles were broken. Ropes, climbing gear, backpack, and clothing were scattered along the way.

Jim urged Dave to save himself, saying that Dave could make it if he'd abandon Jim. But Dave said, "We leave together."

On the morning of the 24th, an avalanche completely buried Jim. He struggled in pain and fought for air. Dave was buried chest deep, but managed to dig free and rescue Jim again. This time, the avalanche snatched one of their good sleeping bags.

Again Dave dragged Jim to a more protected site. He tunneled a trench and set up the tent across the avalanche chute, with a crevasse uphill from them. He thought the crevasse would swallow up any avalanches coming down the slope.

They heard, then felt, the next avalanche. It rushed down the slope, rocketed across the crevasse, and blasted them down the hill in their tent. The accompanying rush of air ripped the tent floor out, strewing their gear. They came to rest after being thrown about fifty yards.

IN THE EARLY HOURS of the 25th, Dave dug a trench, and he and Jim shared a sleeping bag, bivouac sack, and insulated pad. Dave then summoned the strength to fashion a sled. He placed Jim on it and then began dragging him along their original route on a 45-degree slope. They took only the stove, one and a half freeze-dried meals, and their snow shovel.

The new snow was so deep that Dave was forced to shovel a trail. He shoveled thirty yards at a time, then packed the trail and dragged Jim's sled down it. The process was unending: Dave dragged Jim to the end of the trenched trail, shoveled another thirty yards, packed it down, returned for Jim, then shoveled another thirty yards.

Another avalanche struck, burying Jim. Dave dug him out. Another avalanche struck, burying Dave chest-deep. He managed to hang onto the shovel. Jim talked to him, encouraging him to dig himself out. Dave eventually got free.

For seventeen numbing, exhausting hours, Dave broke trail through the snowfield and over snow-bridged crevasses. They finally stopped for the night, nestled in a trench and snuggled into the sleeping bag with the Gore-Tex bivy sack inside.

On the 26th, Dave continued trailbreaking toward a ramp leading to the Ruth Glacier. They were two-thirds of the way across the final slope when snow released from above and shot toward the climbers. The mass of snow swept them off their feet and hurled them into space.

When they stopped, they found themselves on a narrow ledge — inside a crevasse. There was nothing but blackness below. The surface of the glacier was thirty feet above them. Dave and Jim looked at each other.

In one of those unexplainable responses to disaster, an overwhelming amount of pent-up emotion erupted from both men in the form of uncontrollable laughter. When they recovered from this sudden fit, they spotted a nearby ramp that appeared to lead to the surface. They crawled to the ramp. Half an hour later they emerged, crawling cautiously, back onto the surface of the glacier.

Dave slogged down the slope to the Ruth Glacier with Jim in

tow. He finally just stopped and waited. They were now away from the mountain and back on the main part of the Ruth Glacier. Hours passed, and late in the afternoon the skies cleared.

THEY HEARD AN AIRCRAFT. An H-3 helicopter came into view and quickly landed. Among the people on board was Nick Palmer, an avalanche expert and friend of the climbers.

Rescuers examined the battered men, and the flight crew loaded them into the chopper for the flight to Talkeetna. They flew from there in a larger helicopter to Providence Hospital in Anchorage.

Jim was treated for severe concussion and a broken hip and underwent surgery to repair damage to his right femur. He required a few weeks in the hospital. Dave was treated for frostbitten hands.

While on the mend, the climbers had time to marvel at their survival. They relived their adventure in the comfort of warm rooms, knowing that by rights they should never have returned alive.

A year later Dave received the Carnegie Medal for heroism. But the prize he valued most was his friend's life. ∎

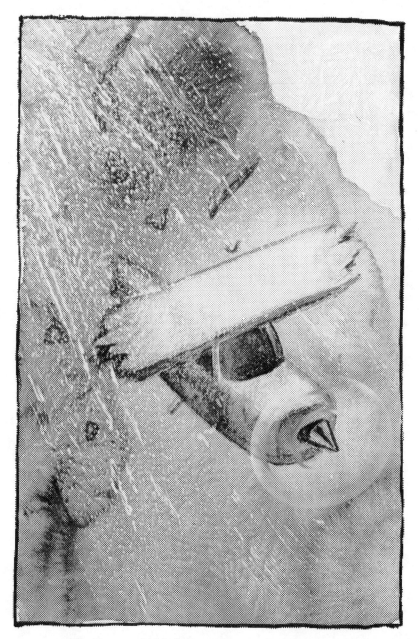

The Cessna skidded across the snow and hit rocks.

4

The Jaws of Death

Waiting for daylight through a February night in Alaska can seem to take forever. I thought about family and friends. They were probably beginning to feel that my chances of survival were dim.

Mike Harbaugh shook his head, rubbed his eyes, and puzzled at the stark scene before him. Snow flurries pelted his exposed skin. Bone-chilling wind pummeled him. He got to his knees, lost his balance, tumbled forward, and started rolling downhill. When he stopped, he saw what remained of his aircraft. Red and white chunks of the Cessna 182 littered the ground. Gradually Mike remembered what had happened.

W E WOKE UP that Sunday, February 9, 1986, to cloudy skies in Flat, Alaska, 300 miles northwest of Anchorage. We wondered if we could make it today. I listened to the radio at the cabin with my friend Glen, a retired Assembly of God minister. The weather forecast was for partly sunny skies.

We went outside and took a look. Even though the wind was up a bit, the ceiling was reasonable — forty-five hundred to five thousand feet. Since Merrill Pass summit is about thirty-five hundred feet, we felt we'd have adequate clearance.

We had been waiting since Tuesday, and we were eager to get to Soldotna. I had gone to Flat to help Glen in exchange for a little bit of equipment and an engine. In the process of helping Glen ferry some things to Soldotna I would return with the engine.

After waiting for four hours for the weather to improve, we decided to take off.

We fired up our two Cessna 182s. I took off first in my 1957 model, but about twenty miles out of Flat, Glen passed me in his newer aircraft. I lost sight of him after that but didn't think anything about it since his plane cruises ten to fifteen miles an hour faster than mine.

Flying over the Kuskokwim Mountains toward Merrill Pass, I was pushing a heavy headwind. It took longer than usual to reach Merrill Pass, our chosen route through the Alaska Range. I hadn't had any radio contact with the FAA, so I didn't have a weather briefing.

I assumed Glen's plane had made it on through the pass. I tried to reach him on the radio but got no response. Buffeted by increasing winds that slammed snow off my windshield from every direction, I fought the controls. The ceiling was still up around five thousand feet. As I entered the pass, I felt confident I could make it through without incident, even though the turbulence bounced me around pretty good.

As I neared the summit, I was surprised to find it socked in with blowing snow. Approaching the Razor's Edge, that section of the pass flanked by sheer rock walls, I scanned the summit for an opening. *Maybe I can squeeze through,* I thought. Visibility was negligible, so I did a 180-degree turn and flew back to the mouth of the pass.

On the return I did some soul searching. I was thinking, *Fuel's low. I'll take another look at the summit. Maybe the weather's cleared a path.* I applied left rudder, left aileron, and banked into the pass.

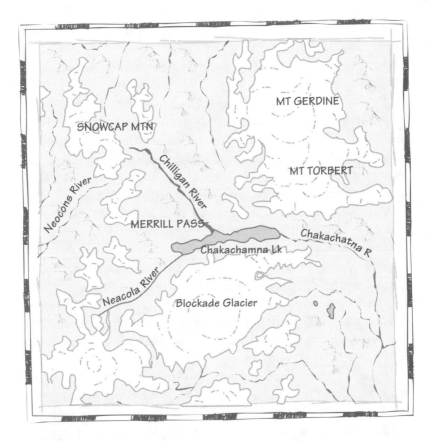

Pilots familiar with Merrill Pass know its history. More than a dozen airframes dot the pass, a graveyard of planes sucked into the walls by wind shear or by the inexperience of the pilot.

I approached the summit again at about forty-five hundred feet. There was no opening. I decided to fly a little closer to confirm the situation. It was immediately obvious I couldn't get through, so I banked to leave the pass. It was around three o'clock.

A large pinnacle rock guards the summit. As I came out from behind that rock, I looked back down the pass, and everything was going fine.

Then I woke up.

THE LAST THING I remember was flying a thousand feet above the pass and coming around the pinnacle. When I banked into the turn, I was at forty-five hundred feet elevation. In a microsecond I lost a thousand feet.

Probably bought the farm on a wind shear, I thought later. *That pinnacle sheltered me from the wind. But as soon as I came from behind it, that mountain wave coming over the summit sucked me down and gobbled me up.*

By the time I gained consciousness and started to figure out what had happened, it was about 5 p.m., with darkness an hour and a half away. At first I didn't realize anything was wrong. I didn't hurt. It was just like a new day. I looked around. I was sitting out in the snow with wind blowing in my face. It didn't look like Soldotna. It sure wasn't my airstrip in Wasilla.

I noticed the pinnacle a quarter of a mile away. Eventually it came to me that I was on the west side of the summit of Merrill Pass.

Though the area of the crash looked steep, my Cessna 182 was not near cliffs. It was toward the bottom of the pass on the only fairly level spot in the summit area. The Cessna had just skidded across that bench, hit rocks, and shed pieces of airplane as it went until it dumped me out into the snow. I was on the uphill side of the fuselage, some fifty feet away.

I saw my coveralls, down mittens, and parka hood out in the snow. I put on the extra clothes and started to drag myself down to the fuselage. But I was now feeling pain so intense that I blacked out again. When I came to, it was starting to get dark. I was getting wet lying in the snow. I managed to drag myself the rest of the way to the fuselage.

I threw a mattress into the fuselage and crawled as far up into the tail as I could to get out of the gnawing wind. I stayed there shivering and awake most of the night, dozing off from time to time.

I realized it was up to me to just wait it out. If the Lord wanted me dead, I'd already be dead. There was a good chance I'd be rescued in the next few days, as soon as the clouds cleared and rescuers could get into the pass. My friend Glen knew my chartered course. I felt confident I'd be found right away.

I worried about my family, knowing they would be concerned when I failed to show up and would have no way of knowing whether I was alive or dead. People lose hope quickly for those who go down in wintertime in Alaska. I didn't want my wife to suffer, thinking I was out here dead or dying. All I could do was pray for my family. I was sure they were praying for me.

As MORNING BROKE, I realized the wind was still coming in the open end of the fuselage where it was sheared off from the baggage compartment. I knew I had to do something.

During the night my eyes had frozen shut, apparently filled with blood from a cut on my nose. In the morning I had to pry them open. I tried to assess my injuries. I had stopped losing blood. My ankle was white and stiff, and I couldn't move it. My collarbone gave me a sharp pain every time I moved. I had some cuts, and my face was messed up. I couldn't feel my teeth with my tongue; I couldn't tell if my teeth were knocked out or just what problems existed in my mouth.

I decided to see if I could find any food or gear. With the injured ankle and collarbone, I couldn't get around too well. Sharp strips of shredded aluminum clung to the fuselage opening; to avoid injury, I crawled out through the baggage compartment door.

My agony and efforts were compounded by the fact that I had lost my boots — I fly without them to better feel the rudder. They were somewhere on the mountain.

I examined the fuselage. The seats had been ripped out, and all the equipment and every piece of paper was gone. *How did I survive?* I wondered. I felt like a shipwreck victim scouring the beach for survival debris.

The plane was scattered for half a mile along the hillside. It appeared the stoves, sleeping bag, food, and everything else had gone down the canyon. I did find a small cardboard box. Not far away was the airplane door.

I wanted to bring my finds back to the fuselage. In agony I pushed the door and the cardboard box back to the airplane. I placed the door across the open part of the aircraft to shelter me from the wind, which continued unabated from the east. I knew I couldn't afford to get any wetter than I was. The temperature was staying in the twenties.

I passed that day trying to figure out ways to stay alive. I opened the cardboard box I had found as if it were a Christmas gift. I actually had no idea what was in it. I was delighted to find wool socks, a dish, rags, and some Tupperware cups. After my down gloves got wet, I used the socks for mittens.

I had read articles describing how Eskimos use oil skins next to their skin to melt snow when they're out on the Bering ice pack. I took a cup, filled it with snow, and put it next to my skin to melt water. It produced a few sips of water every hour or two. I was very dehydrated, and I knew I couldn't go on for long without more water.

I kept thinking of my family: *If I don't make it back, how will they be provided for? I don't have any insurance. We've got no savings to speak of. What will become of them if I don't make it? How will Linda handle the emotional stress, not knowing whether I'm dead or alive? Fortunately we have good friends and a good church; they will take care of her, give her emotional support.*

I rested to conserve my energy. I didn't want to doze off for a long period of time, so I only took cat naps. I tried to stay dry. I was so deathly thirsty by the end of the day that I ate small amounts of snow and ice, even though I knew it would increase the danger of hypothermia.

That night was a long one. Waiting for daylight through a February night in Alaska can seem to take forever. I continued thinking about family and friends. They were probably beginning to feel that my chances of survival were growing dim. I was hoping, and had faith, that someone would find me the next day.

I AWOKE to bad weather. A tremendous wind was blowing the snow off Chakachamna Lake and up into the pass, forming a big whiteout cloud that spiraled upward. Visibility was poor, and a pilot wouldn't be able to see a thing.

That morning I worked a little harder to melt water. I remembered that a generator belonging to Glen was strapped to the floorboard in place of the passenger seat. It probably had some gas in it.

I searched my pockets and came up with some matches. I got my hopes up until I realized the matches had received enough condensation from the blowing snow to get wet. They wouldn't light.

Then I saw that the battery was still in the tail of the airplane. My hands were getting stiff because of cold and exposure, but I managed to remove the cover without any tools. Wiring was still there, running back to my tail strobe light. I thought that with a piece of wire I might get a spark across the positive and negative battery poles. I stripped a piece of wire with my pocket knife, and I got a spark from the battery.

I took a Tupperware dish and crawled up to the generator. I splashed some gas from the generator's tank into the dish and returned to my cubbyhole. I decided to make a fire right on the aluminium floor, hoping to get a little warmth from it and to melt enough snow to make two cups of water.

I cut the cardboard box into small pieces. I felt it would burn pretty good. Holding a piece of cardboard in my fingers, I soaked it in gasoline. I sparked the soaked paper. A small explosion ignited the paper. I burned my fingers, but burned fingers was a small price to pay for a drink of water.

I fed a couple pieces of cardboard onto the fire and it took off. I packed my ceramic cups with snow and placed them as tight to the fire as I could. Eventually the heat rendered a couple of cups of water, and I called it good for the day. I saved the rest of the cardboard and gas so I could melt more water later.

I was becoming weaker. I prayed and again thought about my family, fortifying myself for another long, dark, cold night on the mountain. I prayed that the Lord would assure my family I was still alive. I prayed that God would help the Air Force and the Civil Air Patrol find me.

That night the skies began to clear. With clearing skies, temperatures plummeted. The colder it got, the weaker I became. As I got stiffer and couldn't move, I knew I had to stay awake to survive. I fought sleep.

MORNING DAWNED clear and cold. Though the sheer granite walls of my gray prison seemed to mock me, it was a beautiful spot. Mountains stretched as far as I could see. The azure blue sky was crystal clear. Iced-over waterfalls and pearly white snow and glaciers glistened. Snow covered the ground in places.

I got a perfect view of the perpendicular walls of Merrill Pass. Their very steepness is one reason I didn't mind flying Merrill Pass in the winter. Not much snow sticks to these steep walls, so a pilot gets the benefit of that gray rock contrast in a whiteout. You can almost always see the walls.

I decided to melt some more snow for water. I went through the same process, including burning my fingers. As I worked at melting snow, I was surprised by an airplane flying over. He was so low that I hardly heard him before he passed over. He quickly disappeared down the pass.

The plane looked like a Cessna 180, but my eyes were hurting so badly that I couldn't tell for sure. I thought that perhaps I had gotten some Plexiglas in my eye or that I was suffering from a form of snow blindness.

A few minutes later the plane came around again. I swiftly headed out the baggage door and waved at the plane.

He returned a third time. I was able to focus my vision better. I looked right into the cockpit at the pilot. We made eye contact, and I knew for sure he saw me.

We were a few hundred feet apart at the most. The plane came right down into the pass. I was looking right in the side window at him.

I felt really buoyed and confident that I was going to be rescued.

I dozed off. When I awoke around noon, I heard airplanes overhead. I looked out my door and recognized the bright orange-and-white Beavers of the Anchorage Civil Air Patrol.

I figured the planes were circling the pass as they waited for a helicopter to arrive. I could also hear a C-130 up there. I crawled back into my haven to rest, feeling very good knowing that rescue was only hours away.

By 3 p.m. it had been more than five hours since the first plane flew over. Still no helicopter. I was sure I had been spotted, but I still became a little concerned. I decided to get out and wave at the airplanes. Maybe they hadn't seen me.

Wearing the long wool socks as mittens, I started waving. Nothing happened, so I climbed back into my nest.

Soon after, a small private plane cruised through the pass, low and slow, just as the pilot had done that morning.

I made it to the door, but I didn't have enough strength left to get out of the airplane. All I could do was prop myself up in the baggage compartment and wave. The pilot came through a second time. I looked right in the window at the pilot. I know he saw me.

My hands were swollen and had no feeling. My legs had lost feeling too. But I still had pain that made movement almost impossible.

Now it was dusk, and I heard no more planes. But I knew they had seen me. I figured the helicopter would arrive in the morning. *One more night,* I told myself. *I can make it one more night.*

But about 6:30 that evening I heard the droning of an airplane far overhead. Suddenly a burst of light lit up the canyon

like daytime. It was a parachute flare coming down. It never oc-
curred to me they would come in at night. I had assumed I'd have
to wait until morning.

MIKE HARBAUGH'S disappearance set in place a massive air search
that included Alaska State Troopers and the Civil Air Patrol. On
February 12, the third day of the search, an HC-130 Kingbird
overflew Merrill Pass to coordinate the efforts of thirteen small
private aircraft.

A grueling day of search had revealed nothing. Then word
came to the Rescue Coordination Center at Elmendorf Air Force
Base that Mike Harbaugh had been sighted by two separate pilots,
and he was alive.

Knowing that chances for survival in such severe weather di-
minished by the minute, the rescue team scrambled. Humanitar-
ian concerns dictated a night flight. Major Merle Perrine called
the 71st Aerospace Rescue and Recovery Squadron, requesting a
chopper and crew immediately.

Helicopter pilot Captain Scott Sommer, a veteran of 2,100
hours of flying time, responded with pararescuers Sergeant Ryan
J. Beckman and Airman First Class Patrick Keller. They loaded a
bolt cutter, picks, axes, and medical supplies. Joining them were
the co-pilot, Second Lieutenant Kevin Churchill, and the flight
engineer, Sergeant Richard Proctor II.

The HC-130 Kingbird returned to refuel before joining the
chopper crew in the pass. Crew members of the Kingbird were
excited but apprehensive.

The strategy was for the Kingbird to overfly Merrill Pass, dropping flares to provide light for the helicopter. The two-million-
candlepower four-minute flares would be dropped every three and
a half minutes, the overlap in time ensuring constant light.

The chopper crew's lives depended on the supply of light; it
would be impossible to navigate the gorge in the dark. If the light
failed, it would be tough to climb straight back up the pass without hitting a rock wall.

Blackness engulfed the plane and the helicopter as they
neared their destination. At the site, complications developed
when some of the dropped flares didn't ignite. The chopper hung
in the blackness, fighting air currents and the invisible black
canyon walls.

At one point a flare dropped onto the floor of the Kingbird threatened to ignite a fuel supply, but Senior Airman Bradley Brown kicked it out the door. The flare dropped into the void, cascading light earthward.

Aboard the helicopter, Captain Sommer spotted the downed pilot. The helicopter hovered near the plane's wreckage as Sergeant Beckman prepared to exit. Knifelike arctic wind sliced through the open door as Beckman launched himself onto a snowdrift. He put on snowshoes and crossed the slope to Harbaugh's Cessna.

Beckman called out and reached for the door shield to pull it away. He saw an inert mass bundled against the weather. He radioed to the crew, "He's alive. Send a spine board and cervical collar down with Keller."

THEY COULD HARDLY believe I was alive. I didn't look alive. I figured I would crawl out to them, but I was too weak to move. All I could do was watch them rescue me and enjoy it.

I didn't know they were racing against time and a limited amount of flares. There were no wasted efforts. The two guys ripped the aluminum away from the door and strapped me into a Stokes litter (it was like a sleeping bag on a stretcher; it's real thick and folds over you so they have easy access to you). After securing me, they pulled me through the opening in my plane.

One of the men pressed against me to shield me from the churning rotor wash before signaling for the crew to hoist me. Up I went, into the chopper. After three nights on the mountain I left my tomb, resurrected.

The helicopter crew gave me oxygen and administered intravenous fluids. The helicopter flew toward Anchorage, dangerously low on fuel. It was my first helicopter ride. I was flat on my back, but I was thrilled.

When I arrived at the emergency room, it just so happened that Dr. William J. Mills was there. He is a leading frostbite and orthopedic-bone specialist. His presence further confirmed my belief that my survival and rescue was a miracle by God.

I'd lost thirty pounds. My core body temperature was down to about 80 degrees (and that's after my body had been warmed on the flight into town). It was one of the lowest core temperatures the hospital had ever recorded in a patient who survived.

I was put in the burn unit, where they ran me through the

whirlpools to slowly warm my body. I was completely helpless that first week. After the first three or four days, they managed to elevate my core temperature and got me rehydrated and stabilized.

My leg never hurt me; it had apparently frozen completely. The swelling cut off the circulation and made it freeze fairly quickly, probably eliminating more serious problems. The doctors waited a week to see if I would regain circulation in my leg. I never did. They finally had to amputate the leg.

The hospital's medical staff did a tremendous job in treating me. I got the best care that was available during the three weeks I was in the hospital.

I didn't move around much for six months. I had no money to pay for salvaging my plane. At first the FAA talked like I might have to retrieve the wreck, but eventually I found out I could just let it rest among the other ghost ships in the pass.

Looking back on the rescue, I just praise the Lord that something urged the rescuers to come for me. The night they snatched me from the mountain, the temperature dropped way below zero. I probably wouldn't have made it through the night.

As far as I know, I'm the first crash victim who has ever come away from the summit alive. The same crew that rescued me had removed the bodies from another crash site a few months before my accident. When they found the bodies, brown bears had been feeding on them. This crew didn't want to leave me overnight and come back the next day for a body. They were divinely motivated. ■

The waves increased to fifteen feet and kept building.

5

On Giant Seas

Countless waves rolled alongside the gunwale and pushed the boat to the crest, then suddenly fell away — dropping our small boat twenty-four feet into the trough. The big waves looked like moving mountains.

 When Russ Kommer told his story of survival on Cook Inlet for this book, he felt his experience could serve as a warning to people who head into the inlet aboard small boats. "Sure, you can fish the inlet in small boats," he said, "but it's not a good idea. It's a calculated risk. Sooner or later you're going to get in trouble." Russ should know, as you'll see from the story he tells here.

M Y FRIEND AND COLLEAGUE Mike Siegrist invited me to go halibut fishing in Cook Inlet. He had just bought a sixteen-foot Smokercraft jet boat with high sides. We took it out on a lake one day and ran it a little bit. Everything seemed fine, so we decided it would work okay in the inlet.

Darnell Crosby, the wife of my best friend, had never been fishing, but she said she thought she would enjoy a trip like this. "Well, come along," we told her.

It was the first week in May 1989 — a little early in the season — and it would be colder than during summer fishing. But we figured we were young enough — between twenty and twenty-eight — to endure the cold and any adventure that came our way.

We left at midnight Saturday, after we got off work. We headed south from Anchorage for the 150-mile drive to Deep Creek, where we planned to hit the Cook Inlet high tide so we could put in on the river instead of dragging the boat across the beach.

On the way to Deep Creek, we planned to stop in Kenai to pick up a twenty-five-horse kicker as a backup for Mike's seventy-horse jet unit.

We were partway through Turnagain Pass, which funnels through the mountains between Anchorage and Kenai, when we blew a wheel bearing on the trailer. We finally fixed it and got on the road again.

We stopped in Kenai to buy some herring bait — but we were running late, and we just plain forgot about getting the kicker.

At Deep Creek the water was real nice, as flat calm as you could get. There was a little bit of swell, but we would be able to run wide open with the jet boat. We figured we'd run offshore about two or three miles where most everybody fishes. We put the boat in and took off.

It was a normal Sunday halibut fishing trip: lots of good fellowship, food, and even some halibut we could keep. We enjoyed the camaraderie and continued landing halibut for several hours. A big Grayling jet boat, also out from Deep Creek, fished near us for about an hour and then took off.

THE WATER BEGAN changing. The seas were building. Although rollers were coming in, there was no chop. We had all the fish we needed, and the water was getting rougher, so we decided to start

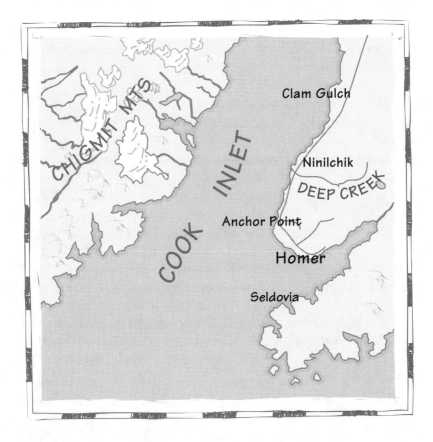

back on the thirty- to forty-minute run to the beach. Meanwhile the Grayling jet boat continued fishing.

Half an hour later, with conditions worsening, we were climbing four-foot swells and crashing down into the troughs. We were running at three-quarters throttle, backing it off when we came to a rougher-than-usual swell.

The flat-bottomed river boat was bouncing badly. Suddenly the motor quit. The water had gotten real choppy, and we were still a mile offshore.

I wasn't too concerned. I thought a gaff hook or something had bounced off the bottom of the boat and crossed out the posts on the battery, killing the engine. But when Mike tried to start the motor, all he got was a click, like a car not quite starting because it wasn't getting enough juice.

I took the engine cowling off and told Mike to hit the key. The starter engaged, but wouldn't turn anything. You could see the flywheel just stop.

I grabbed the flywheel to turn it to see what was causing it to hang up. It wouldn't turn. We hooked a rope onto the flywheel and gave it a big tug, but the flywheel still wouldn't budge; it was frozen solid.

By now we had six-foot seas. We could really have used the kicker that we forgot back in Kenai. We didn't have a radio, and we didn't have flares.

Still I wasn't too worried. I knew the Grayling jet boat was continuing to fish out on the inlet. "That Grayling will be coming in here," I said. "He's got to go into Deep Creek. We'll flag him down."

The seas picked up again real quick, throwing six- to eight-foot waves at us with the tops breaking. Then we heard the Grayling start up — but instead of coming our way, we could hear him running off. He must have decided to run in to Anchor Point to wait out the weather.

It was getting late in the day. We decided to try paddling. I've never thought there's much point trying to get anywhere by paddling in the inlet — but what else were we going to do? Trouble is, we didn't have any paddles.

We took a floorboard out and kicked it in half. With these two pieces of half-inch-thick plywood, Mike and I paddled for hours. We'd move the boat twenty or thirty feet, then have to rest. The tide was going out, so we were fighting the tidal current plus the waves, wearing ourselves out.

As dark came on, we realized we would have to ride the night out. During the night I saw the lights of only one boat, a commercial vessel along Anchor Point, close to the shore and going toward Homer. We drifted all night. The seas grew to eight- and ten-foot swells with chop. I was beginning to think it might be too much to hope that we could survive these wild waters in a flat-bottomed river boat. Darnell, one tough lady, just gritted her teeth and hung in there with us.

ON THE MORNING of the next day, Monday, the waves increased to fifteen feet and kept building to twenty-four feet — higher than the length of the boat. Whenever we dropped into a trough, we could no longer see the mountains; we'd look up at nothing but water.

All day we kept trying to start the motor. The inlet stayed

rough, and we saw no boats. The water built up to even greater seas. The tops of the waves were breaking, and the wind increased. Mike and I took turns bailing, using a coffee can. But now there was six to eight inches of water in the bottom all the time.

We had plenty of food and water aboard: five-gallon water jugs, fried chicken, sandwiches, and soda pop. But we didn't eat very much; we were too worried.

We had to consider what would happen if we capsized. There were some life cushions in the boat and we each wore a Stearns flotation vest. *This boat's going to tip over,* I thought. *If we can all get hold of something, at least we won't get separated.* I took parachute cord and ran it through the handles of all the five-gallon gas cans and the cooler. The cans should float and would give us something to hold onto.

To lighten the boat, we threw our ice overboard. We also tossed out the fish — but we kept one nice halibut because it was Mike's biggest fish.

MONDAY NIGHT brought sixteen- to twenty-four-foot seas. It was so rough that we couldn't sit on the seats. The three of us, Darnell in the middle, sat on cushions on the floor to reduce the pounding. We scrunched up under the metal hood that covers the front. Everyone was soaked. We huddled under the bow covering most of the night, hoping that if we kept our body heat together, we could avoid hypothermia.

Countless waves rolled alongside the gunwale and pushed the boat to the crest, then suddenly fell away — dropping our small boat twenty-four feet into the trough. We continually crested and dropped, crested and dropped. Two or three twenty-four-foot waves would make up one monster wave.

The big waves looked like moving mountains. As they rolled alongside the gunwale, they pushed the boat real fast. We leaned into each wave in hopes the boat wouldn't roll. Once a wave went past and the boat dropped, we had to lean the other way. We did that for hours, constantly leaning into the boat, bailing, hoping.

Mist and fog enveloped us. The temperature was forty degrees. We sat in water. Mike and I were wearing hip boots that were full of water, but they still kept our feet warm.

I couldn't keep track of the time because we didn't have a

watch. It was as dark as the inside of a cow. In the middle of the night I saw what looked like a hotel coming at us, coming out of the horizon real small and getting bigger and bigger. Mike was dozing; Darnell just had her head tucked and was praying we were going to make it out of there. I kept looking at the approaching light, but I didn't say anything because I didn't want to get everyone's hopes up for nothing.

As the light came closer, I realized it was a Sealand barge heading toward port at Homer. The barge was huge, with semi-trailer boxes stacked on it. We were right in its path. *This thing's gonna run us over,* I thought.

I woke Mike. I tried to start the boat and move us out of the way. The barge was only about three hundred yards away when it changed course enough to miss us. But they hadn't changed course on our account; they hadn't even seen us. I could see the guy in the wheelhouse. But he didn't see us. We shot off our 9-millimeter pistol again and again, but no one noticed. Our hopes soared, then they dropped.

Darnell even asked me, "Are we gonna die, Russ?" I told her that if the boat tipped over, we would die, but that if it stayed up, we could live a long time because we had water and food.

The seas continued rough all night. We kept on with our survival routine: bail water, try to stay warm, lean into the waves to keep the boat upright. Somehow we made it through the night.

A DISTANT CLUNKING gradually pressed into my consciousness. It was very early in the morning. I looked around. It scared me to realize I'd gone to sleep.

The seas were calm, dead calm.

The storm was over. Now there was storm debris all around us on the surface of the water: trees and lots of junk. The clunking sound was a forty-foot tree that was hung up in the jet.

Mike woke up and asked what was going on. "It's calm," I told him. "We're gonna make it out of here today."

I leaned over the gunwale and pushed the log down and away from the jet unit. After three tries we were free from the tree.

With the return of calm seas, Mike and Darnell gave in to their exhaustion and slept. I turned my attention to the jet unit, thinking that loosening the bolts on the jet unit and pulling it down a bit might free something up enough to get it running.

I was shivering, and I knew that was a good sign that I wasn't hypothermic yet. I was really thirsty. I got a can of Mountain Dew soda from the cooler and had just opened it when I received a terrible scare. A sea lion came up right next to the boat.

I woke Mike and told him to give me the gun. I'd heard too many stories of sea lions jumping into a boat and tipping it over. The sea lion was swimming near the boat and barking. What scared me was that a halibut was in the boat, and the lion might smell it and come right up over the side for the fish. Mike was still groggy. He handed me the gun and said, "It's not loaded."

"Well, you better load it 'cause there's a sea lion here," I said.

Mike looked up, got the pistol, and jacked a shell into it. The sea lion dove under the boat and come up on the other side. We shot two or three times into the air. We could tell by its reaction that it knew what guns were, but we still had to shoot two clips of shells before it finally left.

Mike and I told Darnell to keep moving to try to warm up her feet. They were freezing, and the veins were so cold that they were collapsing.

We went back to work on the jet unit. I hung over the back and loosened the nuts. We hit the starter and pulled the rope on the flywheel at the same time. The motor started, moved the boat twenty feet — and stopped. We kept trying for a couple of hours, and the motor kept starting and then stopping.

A thick fog covered the water. We heard boats off in the distance, but we couldn't see them. The fog burned off as the sun rose. We heard an outboard motor, and a mile away we saw a Zodiac inflatable coming from Homer. This was a good sign, because if this craft was out on the water, we knew conditions were pretty nice between us and Homer. The Zodiac just kept on going down the inlet.

Charter fishing boats started coming out of Homer, and the sound of their engines was encouraging. But we were so far out that we didn't know if they would get out to us.

A couple of charter boats came out and shut down long before reaching our position. We could see the cabins and masts of the charter boats, but they couldn't see our low-sided Smokercraft.

One charter boat finally came out and shut down closer to us. We began firing three shots from the pistol every half hour. Three shots is known as a distress signal. But we got no response. Even if someone heard us, the likelihood of a response was nil because people are accustomed to hearing shots out on the water: people shoot large halibut to kill them before bringing them aboard, commercial fishermen shoot at seals and sea lions, and so on. The sound just goes in one ear and out the other.

We took our landing net and tied a yellow raincoat to it as a flag. I stood as high as I could and waved the makeshift flag as we all yelled. One of the people on the charter boat heard us.

The captain started his boat and came out to us. It was 10 o'clock Tuesday morning.

"Boy, you guys are out here early," he said.

"Yeah, well, we've been here for three days," I told him.

"Do you know how big them waves were?" he asked, suddenly concerned.

"Yep, first hand," I told him.

The boat was the *Billy Joel*, skippered by Jim Thompson. He asked if we wanted to come aboard. This struck me as a strange question, considering our desperate situation, but I guess it's just a question a skipper has to ask.

We came on board the *Billy Joel*, and the people there were just a hundred percent good, and they took care of us.

Thompson called the Coast Guard, and the Coast Guard told our families how we were. The volunteer Coast Guard at Homer sent out its rescue boat *Quanah P.*

Meanwhile, Thompson shut everything down and the people on the boat went back to fishing. A couple of hours later the rescue boat showed up and took us aboard. We were trying to keep Darnell warm, so we put her in a bunk. The Coast Guard vessel brought our boat along.

We had to help Darnell to the dock at Homer because she was unable to walk, and an ambulance came for her. The doctor who treated her said she was suffering from trench foot because of exposure to the cold and wet. It took several months, but her feet eventually recovered.

WE MADE IT back alive because each person kept calm. We all maintained good spirits through the ordeal. If just one of us had lost control and done something that would have flipped the boat over, we'd all have been dead.

I've learned a few things from the experience. Now I carry a marine radio, a flare gun and eight or ten flares, a couple of space blankets, and a spare motor.

I don't think you should take a river boat out in Cook Inlet in the first place. They're not made for that. The pounding surf beats the rivets out of the bottom. The flat-bottomed river boat can't take the water as well as a V-bottomed boat because it bounces up and down instead of cutting into the surf.

We got into the problem that we did because we were in too much of a hurry to go fishing. I've heard that in the Coast Guard's training for Cook Inlet rescues, they use us as the bad example, referring to us as the "three out there." In Alaska, if you get in a hurry or don't have the right equipment or aren't prepared, you're asking for big, big trouble. ■

Some of the ducks dropped on the other side of the slough.

6

Underwater Coffin

The plane hit the water and flipped over. My head was underwater instantly. The entire cockpit was full. I didn't have a chance to take a breath.

For teacher Darrel Misner, it was to be a glorious day of duck hunting. But Alaska has a way of throwing surprises into the simplest outdoor activity.

O N OCTOBER 22, 1977, I flew from the airstrip bordering my Ocean View home in Anchorage to go duck hunting. The plan was to hunt the Chickaloon Flats, an area where the Chickaloon River dumps into the Turnagain Arm tidal flats ten miles south of my home.

Getting to the hunting grounds was always quick and easy for me. I would just go out to the backyard, jump in the plane, and take off. I'd be there in about fifteen minutes.

The mud flats are ten miles long, extending west from the base of the Kenai Mountains to where they turn into sand beaches on the shores of Cook Inlet. So there is a large area for duck hunting. I like flying into the mud flats in the fall because they are frozen solid, and you can land and take off easily.

My usual routine is to fly around and spot for ducks for ten minutes and then pick a landing spot a short distance from the birds. Then we start hunting.

I've had my greatest success at Chickaloon hunting the tide guts, which are channels cut through the mud flats by the incoming and outgoing tides. At slack tide, these channels resemble sloughs through the flats. Before the tide is fully in, you can sneak up to the edge of a gut before the ducks can see you. When they flush, you can pop them off.

Some of the ducks we shoot invariably drop on the other side of the slough. It's difficult to retrieve the birds because the mud in the guts is so thick. Walking through the mud is an invitation to get stuck — and when the tide comes in, the water is over your head.

A good dog could retrieve the ducks and reduce the danger. But we don't use a retriever; we get the ducks with my plane. I just jump in the plane, crank it up, fly to the other side of the gut, and retrieve the ducks.

Because of the sticky mud, I wear hip boots over my pants when I hunt. I usually roll them down so they're just like a regular boot. On that day I was also wearing a wool shirt, a full-length Frostline down jacket, gloves, and a toque — a knit hat. I was accompanied by another hunter, a tall, lanky veterinarian from Palmer.

The temperature was right around freezing in the morning, which meant it would be thawing in the afternoon. The barometric pressure was one of the lowest in years, and the winds were squirrelly.

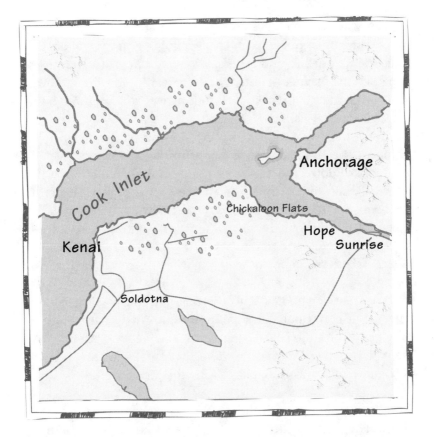

We landed and hunted a tide gut that was about 100 feet wide. The hunting was fantastic.

THE FIRST SIGN that this was not going to be just another routine day of hunting cropped up when I went to retrieve some ducks. We had shot the ducks and I prepared to fly to the other side of the gut to get them. The plane carried the usual load: full gas tanks, survival gear, a sleeping bag or two, and my tools.

We were on a strip of mud flat about a thousand feet long. I usually only need two or three hundred feet to get airborne. I decided against taking off right down the strip because the winds just didn't seem to be right. Instead I took off perpendicular to the mountains. The plane didn't jump into the air as usual; it felt sluggish.

I landed on the other side of the gut, picked up the ducks, took off again, and landed back where I started. We hunted for a while longer and then prepared to leave.

I performed a preflight check, looking at the fuel for possible water contamination, inspecting the landing gear for any damage from sticks or debris, and generally looking the plane over. Inside I checked the magnetos, tested the carb heat for maximum power, pushed the rudders to make sure nothing was jamming, and tested the ailerons and flaps.

The winds were swirling about, blowing ten to fifteen miles an hour. The temperature was about thirty-five degrees.

I looked down the thousand-foot mud flat, noting that it had no chuckholes or obstructions. At the very end was a patch of grass, not far from the water. We taxied down the strip, building speed for takeoff, but the plane didn't gain a lot of momentum. It just kept going and going. My flying experience spoke to me: *When we hit that little patch of grass, just accelerate and we will take off.*

We were perpendicular to the tide gut and parallel to Cook Inlet on takeoff. I pulled the tail down and tried to get up in the air when we hit the edge of that grass, and we were airborne. We went twenty-five feet or so beyond the grass, right out over the tide gut, which was now filling with the incoming tide.

ONE SECOND we were in the air; the next instant we were in the water. The plane hit the water and went over backward, upside down. My head was underwater instantly. The entire cockpit was full. I didn't have a chance to take a breath. Because the tail went over more slowly, my passenger had time to take a breath just before going under.

In the murky water, I couldn't see a thing. I couldn't tell if I was sitting up, or was on my side, or was upside down. I hit the quick-release on my shoulder harness. I panicked. In my frantic actions I knocked my glasses off. My hands were going ninety miles an hour — feeling for the windshield, feeling for the side, feeling for the doorknob, trying to get out.

I couldn't find the door latch. I tried to go out through the windshield, but it was still intact. I don't know how much time elapsed. It seemed like forever. I kept moving my hands around frantically, but time seemed to crawl in slow motion.

Suddenly I started inhaling water, gulping a little bit. Then I consciously didn't do anything. I went totally limp. I didn't move my hands. I didn't move anything, not a muscle. That's when I could feel myself being slightly lighter, floating back and forth a little bit. What ran through my mind was, *This is what it's like to drown. This is what it's like to drown.*

I don't know how it happened, but somehow I reached out calmly and found the doorknob. I opened the door and popped out of the cockpit like a cork.

I hit the surface, with my passenger right behind me. He'd shot through the door with me. He had tried to go out through the fabric in the side, but couldn't break through. Trapped in the back seat, he couldn't get out until I opened the door.

The water in the tide gut was over our heads. We stood on the plane's wing, in neck-deep water, all blue and coughing. We couldn't have survived underwater much longer. A few inches of the plane's tires pointed skyward out of the water.

I considered diving back into the plane to get my emergency locator transmitter. But I probably wouldn't have made it. My companion had noticed a Cessna 150 circling above, so we knew another plane had seen us go in.

The tide was coming in fast and we had to get off the wing. In the upper part of Cook Inlet, big tides roll in. In only a matter of minutes, the whole plane was covered.

We struggled to shore, wading and swimming. We got down on the side of a tide gut and huddled together, trying to find cover out of the wind. Since we'd been seen and we weren't far from Anchorage, we knew we would be rescued soon. We huddled in the tide gut and waited. Then our knees began shaking violently, uncontrollably.

As the tide swelled in, it pushed us out of our protected spot in the gut. And there was no other protection. After an hour of huddling in the wind, we began walking toward some cabins that I knew were two miles away.

We had walked about halfway when we heard the unmistakable *wop, wop, wop* of a helicopter, a beautiful sound. It was a big military chopper, and its blades kicked up so much wind that, as cold and numb as I already was, I became even colder.

Rescuers jumped out of the helicopter with blankets to cover us. They carried us back to get on board; we couldn't move by ourselves because of our numbness from the cold.

It was warm in the helicopter. They got us out of our wet clothes and into dry clothes and then into sleeping bags. We were saved, after the most adventurous day of duck hunting I ever hope to have.

LATER I HAD the luxury of analyzing the accident. I realized I probably should have shut the engine down when we had so much trouble gaining speed before liftoff. Then I could have tried something else. But instead I banked upon past experience, thinking that I could simply hit the little patch of grass just before the inlet, accelerate, and be airborne. The crash could have been caused by a combination of things, including the low barometric pressure, the squirrelly winds, and perhaps even an inadvertent push by my passenger on the brakes beneath the pilot's seat in front of him.

I managed to salvage the engine, fuselage, and one wing before the tides took the rest of the plane out to sea. I cleaned the salvaged parts and sold them.

I've now got another Super Cub on my backyard airstrip. I've made some adjustments since my dip in the inlet, which I like to think of as my only saltwater baptism. I wear a helmet now when I fly. And the plane's shoulder and seat harnesses are more securely fastened to the fuselage or the frame. I'm a firm believer that a shoulder harness will save ninety percent of the lives in plane accidents.

The gas tanks of my plane are always topped off with fuel, my survival gear is safely stowed with my tools, and I'm ready to go at a moment's notice. I love seeing those green-headed mallards set their wings over the Chickaloon Flats, and I want to keep *my* wings intact so I can join them when the cottonwood and aspen trees turn gold in October. ∎

Because I was between his antler palms, he couldn't get his tines into me.

7

On the Horns of a Bull

As I approached the bull moose, I noticed a hind leg begin to contract. The wounded bull started to get up. With only twenty feet separating us, I turned and ran. My feet outran my body and I fell down. I started to get up just as the bull's entire weight rammed into my back.

Mark Hewkin and his hunting buddies had honed their archery skills as they eagerly antici- pated the Alaskan moose season. And after it was over, he talked about the hunt that saw a moose turn the tables on his hunter.

JOHN SCHNEIDER put together our Alaska hunt in the fall of 1987. Our group included John's brother-in-law Jamie Lane, who had accompanied him on other big game hunts, and Mike Mitten, who asked me to be his partner. John is a carpenter, Jamie is an insurance salesman, Mike is a lab technician, and I am a laborer for a sewer and water company. We were all twenty-nine or thirty years old and married with children, except for John. All live in Illinois, except Jamie, who hails from South Dakota.

Bow hunters, we had a combined hunting experience of sixty-two years. Our kills included mule deer and elk as well as a number of animals recorded in the Pope and Young Record Book: twenty-seven white-tailed deer, two black bear, and three antelope.

John called several flying services in Alaska to determine whether we would book a guided trip or a drop camp where we would be on our own to float and hunt a stream. We favored a float-hunt but were told that the trophy animals we sought would be well back from the river because of hunting pressure. Ultimately we chose a drop-camp hunt where we would have the opportunity to hunt from a base camp without the hassle of constantly hiking off the river in pursuit of quality animals.

After much inquiry we settled on High Adventure Air Charter, a Soldotna-based flight service located on the Kenai Peninsula and only fifty air miles south of Anchorage.

The owner of High Adventure Air, Sandy Bell, assured us that we would have adventure during our hunt from August 28 through September 18. We planned to hunt caribou for six days and moose the rest of the time. A pilot would check on us one time in caribou camp and one time in moose camp.

Bright and early on the morning of August 28 we drove to the airstrip at Soldotna, stopping on the way to buy the licenses we needed. Sandy's son Greg, a twenty-four-year-old seasoned pilot, stowed our gear into a DeHavilland Beaver floatplane. The gear included two tents, one stove, sleeping bags, side arms, backup bear medicine (a 12-gauge shotgun and a .30-06), and compound bows and arrows.

Our first destination was the west side of Lake Clark, about a hundred miles west of Soldotna. We flew through Lake Clark Pass, bypassing several glaciers and snowpacked mountain peaks. Greg pointed out several caribou along the way before landing on a small lake nestled among three large lakes.

The surrounding area was rocky and looked lifeless. Rolling hills dappled with alder thickets pushed up to two thousand feet. Many small scattered ponds accentuated a moonlike landscape.

We eagerly set up camp, excited about the days ahead. We planned to seek caribou by hiking in a large circle that would get us high enough to see the area and yet bring us back to camp each day. Little did we realize that we would be covering fifteen to twenty miles a day.

On the second day, Mike stalked a bedded bull caribou near a sandy-beached pond. He sneaked within ten feet of the bull and arrowed it. The animal jumped to its feet and ran. Mike hit it again and dropped it. His first arrow hit the shoulder and the second penetrated the lungs. We headed back to camp, planning to retrieve the meat the next day. Back at camp, we saw signs that a grizzly had wandered through camp in our absence.

The next morning I spotted three bulls, and I got within twenty-five yards of one of them. As he quartered away from me,

I placed an Easton 2219 arrow tipped with a Zwickey broadhead in his rib cage behind his left shoulder, the shaft stopping abruptly against the right shoulder blade. He went eighty yards before he piled up. I returned to camp for Mike's help, and we carried most of the meat to camp in our first trip.

Then Mike and I went to get his dead caribou. We found that a bear had picked it up and carried it about seventy-five yards over a hill and into the open. We mustered the courage to approach the kill with only knives for defense, but the bear was nowhere in sight. Mike's caribou looked like it had been hit by a truck. It was smashed flat and skinned. Every part of its body had been eaten on, and two-thirds was completely consumed. We salvaged only about sixty pounds of meat.

Meanwhile our buddies had sneaked to within eighty yards of a bull that would score very high for the size of its antlers, but they didn't connect. That turned out to be the last caribou we hunted, and we flew out of caribou camp September 2. Since we had not seen many caribou, we were a pretty disgusted group of hunters.

WHILE FLYING to moose camp we spotted several of the big animals, two of them very impressive. We touched down on a shimmering, gray-blue lake at the base of snowclad mountains draped halfway up with alders, willows, and black spruce — truly the prettiest place I have ever seen.

While the rest of us set up camp, Mike ascended the hill behind our site, scouting for a suitable route the next morning. He saw three grizzlies, which didn't excite us. Their presence meant we'd probably see more of them and possibly have problems with them.

Next morning Mike and I headed south while John and Jamie went north. From the hilltop we saw six cow moose and several caribou. We stopped at a thousand-foot-deep gorge; it was the major obstacle to hunting the opposite side, which we planned to do the following day.

The next day, however, my partner left without me because I was sick; my hypoglycemia was acting up. My symptoms included blurred vision, headache, stomach sickness, and nausea.

Four and a half hours later, Mike reached the area beyond the gorge. His efforts were rewarded when he saw nine moose: seven cows and two bulls. Mike focused on a bull with an antler spread of some sixty-five inches. He crawled to within forty yards and got off an arrow, but it was high.

By this time Mike was so exhausted he just lay on the ground, wondering if he could make it back to camp. He looked up and saw a lone grizzly feeding on blueberries 150 yards away. It was one of seven grizzlies Mike saw that day. Sighting that bear gave Mike new motivation to get back to camp.

John and Jamie had seen some cows that day, and they also spotted a bull they had seen before, one they had nicknamed Hal. They determined to get Hal the following day. But we were learning that plans change. The following day we remained in camp to recuperate. John needed to rest his legs, which gave us an excuse to catch sockeye salmon and to watch Hal through our spotting scope.

Before daylight next morning Mike and I headed for the gorge. The first light we saw was at the top of the hill, and it was accompanied by a sea of fog. By noon the fog was so thick we could see only fifty yards. Wet and cold, we returned to camp to discover our partners had seen the fog roll in and stayed in camp all day.

It rained almost every day. The temperature was in the low thirties during the nights and the mid-fifties during the days.

Mike and I went to the gorge the next day. Mike saw two bull moose, one of which was below us on a near-vertical slope a half mile away. The other one was 500 yards away. We focused on the closer one and began our stalk. Because of the steepness and our rapid descent, Mike hurt his ankle and I hurt my knee.

As we neared the bull, we slowed our pace and our senses intensified. We got into our stalking mode, silently creeping through the head-high willows and around the dead alder stumps. Then we spotted the bull. He was sweat-covered, standing over a scrape, simultaneously urinating and ejaculating into it and pawing the earth with a front hoof; this is the way bulls characteristically leave their scent for cows.

A small bull and a half dozen cows stood nearby. Whenever the young bull approached, the big bull became agitated. We watched for half an hour, unable to improve our position for fear of being spotted. Finally the big bull chased the little one away, giving Mike a chance to make his move.

Mike took a direct path through the alders to within thirty yards before drawing on the animal, which stood free of the brush in an opening. Mike released an arrow that took the bull in the neck. The animal ran ten yards before stopping, presenting Mike another shot. The second arrow entered behind the right shoulder and pierced the animal's lungs. The bull ambled off forty-five yards and dropped dead.

We took some pictures and then started off for the other bull, but we found only cows. So we returned to dress Mike's bull. It carried an antler spread of fifty-six inches, and we guessed he weighed sixteen hundred pounds. We quartered the bull in preparation for packing him out the next day.

We moved our base camp to a lake closer to the downed moose, thus reducing packing time and effort. (We discovered later that the downed moose was thirteen miles from our original camp.) We now had only five days left to hunt. Mike said he would pack the moose out by himself to our new camp, leaving the rest of us free to hunt. But Mike discovered that bears had found his bull and buried it.

We saw moose every day, but we were showing the efforts of our hunting. John's legs hurt badly enough that he had trouble getting around, which was contrary to his contagious spirit of adventure.

Soon we had only two days left before the plane would be coming to pick us up. I spotted and stalked a respectable bull, only to miss it three times from twenty yards.

The day after my miserable performance, we saw lots of bulls, but other than one Jamie stalked and lost, none interested us. Up to now we'd seen twenty-one grizzlies, three black bear, more than thirty cow moose, and twelve bulls, four of which had racks bigger than fifty inches.

OUR SCHEDULED PICKUP date arrived with strong winds; the lake we had landed on had four-foot waves. There was no way the pilot would be able to land and find the note telling him of our move to the new camp.

Sixty-mile-an-hour winds pounded us the following day. We saw our plane go over. At three o'clock I decided to go hunting.

I had two arrows — one of my own and one I'd borrowed from Mike. After I reached the knob of land that gave a good view, I looked through the scope for several minutes. I walked the eighth of a mile to the far end of the knob and sat down.

As I thought about our hunt and about going home, two bulls and a cow appeared from a big draw. I quickly headed for them, dropping my pack as I drew near. I eased into a streambed to help silence any noise and to enable me to speed my approach through alders.

I couldn't detect the animals till I suddenly heard a bull grunting. Fifty yards away, opposite an alder patch, a bull was slapping a tree with his antlers — not rubbing it but actually dismantling it.

I stalked within twenty yards of the grunting bull moose. All I could see was hindquarters. His head and half his body were hidden in the alders. Imitating a big bull, I scraped the brush with my bow and broke off as many branches as possible, trying to "call" him to me. Then I learned I'd stalked the smaller of the two bulls.

Now where is his big brother? I asked myself, starting in the direction I expected to find the larger bull. I spotted him and stopped behind a spruce tree. His rack stood out above an alder patch forty yards away.

I began breaking limbs and rubbing the tree with my bow, working the tree and grunting. The bull would have none of it. I recalled a sound Mike's bull had made when approaching a cow, and I imitated it. The bull instantly acknowledged me and walked straight toward me.

When he was five yards away, I tried to draw my bow string. I was so excited I couldn't pull it back. The bull turned and trotted toward the alders. I finally got the string to the corner of my mouth and launched the arrow. A 2219 Easton aluminum arrow thwacked into the back of his rib cage, striking bone. Half the shaft stuck out his side as he vanished into the brush. *I'll give the bull half an hour to die before tracking it,* I thought.

Now the waiting game, the suspense. As time passed, I decided to play some games with the little bull. Standing behind a tree, I rubbed it with my bow, breaking limbs and trying to sound big. I was making one low-volume grunt. Then I made the sound Mike's bull had made when approaching a cow, and the bull came right to me.

I grunted and put my bow on my head, trying to imitate him, but he would neither give ground nor advance on me. He just stood there drooling, never more than twenty yards from me. His rack measured forty-five to fifty inches. I'm sure he would have made the record books. But still he was small compared with the bull I had just shot.

I started after my prize, the wounded bull. There was no blood, but his tracks were easy to follow. I crawled through the alders until I spotted him forty yards away, standing and slowly twisting his head from side to side. I drilled him through the neck with another arrow. Blood poured down his neck as he charged into some spruce trees and disappeared.

A couple of minutes later I went to the spot where I'd last seen him. My arrow had gone through him: I found it sticking out of the moss. I picked it up and continued pursuing him.

I hadn't taken two steps when the bull jumped up fifteen yards away and ran directly in front of me. I shot again, striking him behind the shoulder. Half the arrow was showing as the bull vanished into the brush.

Since the bull wasn't far away and it would be easy to come back with help the next day to find his body, I started back to camp. When I reached the top of the hill, I took a look and saw the bull lying on the ground, immobile. I was elated that he was dead and decided to examine my trophy. It was only five o'clock, so I still had plenty of daylight left. Back down the hill I went.

As I APPROACHED the bull, I noticed a hind leg begin to contract. The bull started to get up. With only twenty feet separating us, I turned and ran. My feet outran my body and I fell down. I started to get up just as the bull's entire weight rammed into my back.

He hit me high in my left buttock, his horn piercing the cheek. He pushed me ten feet across the ground, then flung his head upward. I flew off his antlers into the air and came down astraddle his forehead. My arms shot out and around either side of his antlers, and I wrapped my legs around his nose.

I'm going to die! I thought. *I'm going to die!*

I hung on for dear life.

My next thought was, *If I get off his horns, he'll gore me to death.*

He kept ramming his head into the ground until my weight proved too much. He knelt down to rest and then tried again to gore me or shake me off. He continued to smash me into the ground.

Because I was between his antler palms, he could not get his tines into me. He was so weak that his forelegs were nearly buckling.

I was exhausted. My arms and back ached, and it required total concentration to hang on. I was looking into the bull's eyes. I will never forget his eyes or the smell of his wet hair or the cooing-type sound he was making.

The last time he lunged forward to stand up, he stepped on my left foot. The combination of his weight on my foot and his pulling back knocked me from his horns. I turned to get out from under him but actually turned into him. He trampled my body from one end to the other, producing the most pain of the entire experience.

I got up and ran. I looked back after thirty or forty yards. The bull had fallen to the ground.

I turned toward camp and started walking. My head and shoulders were covered with blood, much of which was from the moose. My nose was bleeding. I felt a hole in my buttock cheek and gauged its size by inserting three fingers. I pressed my left hand against it to apply pressure as I walked. Blood kept running down my leg. I was afraid of bleeding to death. I had cuts from sticks and tree limbs where the bull had slammed me around.

Although I didn't think I was going to live, I never gave up or gave in. I just wanted to get back to camp and help. I stopped at three different creeks to drink water and kept moving toward camp. Walking wasn't too difficult, but the bleeding and the thought of dying plagued me.

I was worried about encountering a grizzly. I smelled like a fresh moose steak.

TWENTY MINUTES from camp I saw Mike and Jamie. I told them what had happened and asked them not to touch me because I wasn't sure what injuries I had. At camp, Mike got out the first-aid kit, and the guys worked on me. They found an entry hole and an exit hole in my left buttock cheek. The bull's horn had entered the center and exited the upper left side of the cheek.

They stuffed gauze into the two holes, packed them to stop the bleeding, and taped up the wound. My nosebleed had stopped. I had a couple of small cuts and bruises around my eyes. My arms and back were bruised pretty bad. They gave me Tylenol with codeine, and that night they periodically replaced the gauze as blood saturated it.

The following morning I was hurting all over. To lie in one

position for more than a couple of minutes caused excruciating pain. My bruises hurt a lot more than the holes in my buttock. While I lay in agony awaiting our pilot's return, Mike and Jamie retraced my steps to find my gear and the moose.

Our pilot, Greg, flew over that day on his way to our original drop-off site. He flew over our former camp for five or ten minutes, but returned to Soldotna because it was too windy to land.

Four hours later Mike and Jamie returned with my backpack. They found nothing else.

Several planes flew over on the following day, and my partners tried to flag them down. Finally in late afternoon, Larry Van Slyke, a pilot and officer for the National Park Service, saw them waving, and he landed to help.

Larry and his partner helped me into their Skywagon and flew me to Port Alsworth on Lake Clark while my partners waited back in camp. Larry's wife made me some dinner while Larry arranged to have me flown to Soldotna.

Finally, back in Soldotna, I was picked up at the airport by another of Sandy's sons, Dave. He took me to their home, got me some clean clothes, and took me to the hospital. The hospital staff cleaned my wounds — the puncture in my buttock was two inches deep and an inch and a half in circumference — and then sent me on my way.

Meanwhile Greg had landed his plane and spent that night on a small lake not far from our camp. He found our note telling that we had changed camps. He found my partners and flew them back to Soldotna the next day, where we were all reunited after a hunting trip that I'll never forget. ■

Our stretch of the Big Su was considered treacherous.

8

The Lure of Devils Canyon

The boat slammed into the canyon wall. I fell off the controls, landing on my knees. I felt that it was all over. I found myself thinking, "I don't know if the boat will survive. There's no way I'm going to get control."

People said you'd be a fool to risk the whitewater hell of Devils Canyon. These immense roiling waters of the upper Susitna River in southcentral Alaska had taken the lives of others who challenged them. Could the river be run upstream, by jockeying a jet boat against the force of the rapids? Steve Mahay had watched others try and fail. Now he was ready to dare it for himself.

M Y WIFE KRIS AND I said goodbye to Denver, Colorado, in
1972 and aimed our Volkswagen Super Beetle up the Alcan
Highway toward Alaska. Eager to find land, we studied the country around Talkeetna, a community established in the early 1900s
to supply trappers and miners.

About 600 people now live in this frontier town, which has
become a staging area for fishermen, tourists, and Mount McKinley
climbers. Situated at the confluence of the Talkeetna, Chulitna,
and Susitna rivers, Talkeetna is the gateway to 200 miles of remote river for sport fishermen who come for king salmon, silver
salmon, and trout.

Kris and I rode the Alaska Railroad out of Talkeetna, parallel-
ing the Susitna (which is often called the Big Su, to set it apart
from the Little Susitna River). Ten miles north of town we got off,
climbed a bluff, and beheld a spectacular view of the Susitna River
with Mount McKinley and the Alaska Range in the background.
We'd found heaven on earth.

We staked out ten acres, filed on it, and built our wilderness
home. I hunted, fished, and trapped. One summer I worked on the
railroad along the river. But all the while, the river piqued my curi-
osity. As a teenager, I had taught whitewater boating at a youth camp.
I had competed in whitewater races. I'm also a diver; a real water-
type person. Our stretch of the Big Su was considered treacherous by
the local people, yet I kept thinking that it could be navigated safely.

A couple of river charter operators offered a modest guiding
service for sport fishermen, mainly working areas near the village
— not as far upriver as our cabin. In 1975 I bought a sixteen-
foot river boat with a twenty-horse Mercury outboard motor and
started exploring the rivers near us. I found that we could safely
navigate them.

In 1977 I started a regular commercial operation, and I continued roaming the local river systems. My explorations sometimes
seemed almost Columbus-like: over the years, we'd seen only three
or four boats go very far up the Susitna, and people railed against
the wisdom of being on those waters.

In 1978 I paid $17,300 for my first large inboard jet boat, a
twenty-four-foot Almar with a 460-horsepower Ford engine. Using the powerful craft I discovered that the Susitna River up to
the base of Devils Canyon could be safely navigated. I initiated a
daily commercial trip up into Devils Canyon.

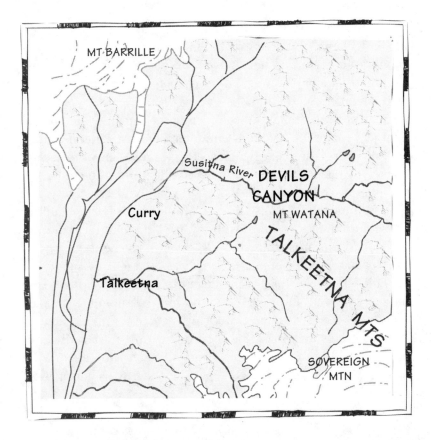

People thought I was crazy, but our clients loved it. We left Talkeetna in the morning with up to ten passengers and navigated sixty-five miles upriver to Devils Canyon and back down again. My clients called the trip through whitewater and unparalleled beauty one of their great experiences. Each time I piloted up into the canyon, I would poke a little bit farther to see how the boat handled through the rocks, standing waves, and complex hydraulics.

MY MIND CONTINUED to tease me, telling me that this canyon could be run, from bottom to top, in a jet boat. In 1983 powerboater Glenn Woolridge challenged the canyon from the bottom. He lost his boat and barely escaped with his life.

Whitewater kayakers also set their eyes on the canyon and its Class VI waters. Kayaker Black Adair is credited with successfully descending Devils Canyon in 1978. Other attempts — including downstream by kayak and upstream by powerboat — were made in the 1980s. A couple of kayakers died.

I studied the stories of these adventures, and I talked to Glenn Woolridge after his failed expedition. I felt that current technology in jet boating had not been put to effective use — and that with more careful planning, I'd have a better chance of making it than Glenn had.

One of the essentials for conquering the canyon would be the right jet-propulsion system. Glenn attempted the canyon using a jet unit with a three-stage, high-speed pump designed for racing; it takes a while for this pump to develop its thrust. The other key essential, of course, was the boat. I owned both essentials for a successful ascent of Devils Canyon. My Almar jet boat — built of 50/51 aluminum — coupled with my 1031 Hamilton jet pump — the best for instantaneous thrust — were fit to the task.

The spring and summer of 1985 was a time of preparation. I flew the canyon in fixed-wing aircraft early in the spring before the ice went out and periodically during the summer. I walked portions of the canyon ridge, studying the rapids through binoculars. (You can't walk the shore because the canyon walls rise hundreds of feet.) I monitored the three rapids that had presented the biggest obstacles to kayakers, expecting these to be my biggest problems.

The total upriver trip would be 215 miles — but the challenge was the 11-mile canyon. We airlifted two barrels of fuel to a spot upriver of the canyon. If I ran the canyon successfully, I'd need enough fuel to dash another 150 miles up the Susitna to the Denali Highway, the only place I could pull out.

I wanted to go into the canyon with just enough fuel on board to make it through — with no unnecessary weight. I stripped the boat of every pound of extra weight, including the floorboards and the captain's seat; I'd drive standing up. We tossed anything that I might get hung up on if the boat went over; I wanted to be washed free of the boat.

We reinforced the bottom parts of the windshield with heavy plywood so the windows wouldn't be blown out by the force of the water. (I'd seen jet boats sink as a rush of whitewater blew out the windows and inundated the craft.) We fortified the boat with Styrofoam blocks to help it stay afloat.

I would be wearing a diver's dry suit, a life vest, and a helmet. I intended to survive, even if the boat didn't.

My personal investment in the boat was $30,000. It was not

insured. With the boat and other costs, I was risking about $50,000 and perhaps jeopardizing the business I'd spent years building. So we planned to produce a film about the attempt. We felt that even if we lost the boat, we could come up with a successful film.

A great deal of thought and effort went into planning for my safety during my solo powerboat run. Don Lee of Talkeetna Air Taxi Service would circle at 5,000 feet, providing radio communications to Anchorage. A chopper from Saloy Helicopter, in Wasilla, would fly above me during my entire attack through the boiling whitewater of the gorge. A paramedic trained in cold-water survival would be aboard. A cargo net would be readied to dangle down to me if I needed to be plucked from the water. My own staff would be standing by with a support vessel.

ON THE MORNING of September 24, 1985, I was ready for action at Portage Creek, our staging point right below the canyon. At 11 a.m., I powered into the bottom part of the canyon and headed toward the first of the three worst stretches of whitewater. This was the steep-walled canyon about a mile upstream from Portage Creek.

A mighty flow of water poured in from my right, at a right angle. I maneuvered the boat into the bottom of two large standing waves — mounds of water that stay in one spot, created by turbulence when the river flows over boulders or down a steep drop into a pool.

My plan called for coming from behind a large rock outcropping that created a protected eddy and roaring into the main flow of the river. I had to make a very hard ninety-degree right turn into the flow. The onslaught of water already coming from my right required maximum power on a full right turn. I jumped out from behind the outcropping.

The trick now was to maintain enough power to push upriver but not so much power that the boat would slam into the canyon wall. I held power for about three seconds, motoring toward the wall. Then I slacked off on the power to avoid hitting the wall. I was too late.

The boat slammed into the wall. I fell off the controls, landing on my knees. I felt that it was all over. I found myself thinking, *I don't know if the boat will survive. There's no way I'm going to get control.*

Because I'd reduced the power just before I hit, the boat was kind of swimming by itself in a trough. I jumped back to the controls. The wall actually helped line the boat up parallel with the flow as I held power on to bring the bow around. I was amazed that the boat was OK. The controls still worked; the gauges still operated. So I powered up and found a slight eddy to the right side of the river.

I was now between haystacks — standing waves that are breaking back on themselves. The haystacks rose as high as twelve feet, taller than the boat. I slid to the right side of the trough between haystacks and worked my way up on the right side and to the relative safety of the next expedition staging area.

I COULD NOW pull up to the shore, where my staff and I tied off the boat. I was shocked that I hadn't taken on water and that I'd survived both the cauldron of water and the collision into the canyon wall.

I knew that the remaining parts of the canyon would be tougher than the one I had just scraped through. I thought, *If this first one was this bad, what will the end of the canyon be like? If I just barely made it through the steep-walled canyon, how on earth am I going to make it through the other ones?*

I was thinking, *Do I really want to go ahead with this?*

But then my original resolve returned. The only way this canyon would ever be conquered by a powerboat would be if someone finally says, "When it looks impossible, just keep going."

Nobody had ever made it as far as the second part of the canyon. Earlier attempts had been foiled at the first rapids, which almost got me. I had just become the first person to get this far.

The next gnarly stretch of water was the one called Hotel Rock. The helicopter had landed at the staging area. I boarded and we flew a three- or four-mile stretch of river. I wanted to scout the torrent in segments so I could remember exactly what course to take when I was back down there again, alone in the boat.

From the helicopter I spotted what looked like a relatively easy route to the left of the boulder. Just above that stretch, in a narrow gorge where the helicopter couldn't fly, was a stretch of water punctuated by giant boulders.

Below us, a great standing wave breached the entire seventy-five-foot width of the canyon. The full flow of the Susitna River

— thirteen million gallons per minute — piled up at this spot. I knew I would have to act quickly when I reached the standing wave. Indecisiveness could kill.

I RETURNED to the boat and started upriver. I knew I had to charge the standing wave, take the shock of hitting it, and then just power up and through.

I had my speed up. I hit the wave. The boat just stopped. I ate the windshield, losing two upper teeth on the spot. Although I piled into the windshield, I wasn't knocked out. Instead I was alert and conscious of what was happening. I gripped the controls.

The boat surged into the standing wave and waddled uphill. Roaring water funneled all around me with a near-deafening noise. The boat crested the wave.

Now there was a bit of reprieve. Though the water was anything but calm, it was peaceful compared to the previous tumult. I could gather my thoughts. I felt my teeth with my tongue. Except for the two missing teeth, I wasn't injured. I continued up the river and reached the refuge of the next staging area, where I went ashore.

I NOW HAD ANOTHER chance for a helicopter reconnaissance and for a discussion with my expedition support group. Making it through the standing wave was a big boost to my confidence. But I knew that the worst part of the course still awaited me: a mile-and-a-half stretch that starts out with The Nozzle.

The Nozzle presents big problems to kayakers because there's a keeper — a spot in the flow that traps objects floating downstream. A kayaker can't escape the water power. Water shoots like a nozzle into a big pool, and the only course is right down The Nozzle. Kayakers get sucked down The Nozzle and into the pool, and they are kept under water for a long time.

ONCE AGAIN I boarded my boat and headed up for the last, and hardest, part of the upstream battle. When I reached The Nozzle, I just powered on top of the flow and rode it up.

For the next mile or so I rode the crest on six- to twelve-foot standing waves. I slid back and forth in the trough from one side of the river to the other, picking my way upstream like a salmon trying to find the quieter water in its path. I was met by a constant barrage of frothy, thundering water that was spawned at The Boiling Pot, which would be the last segment I faced, the portion of water I feared the most. The Boiling Pot sits at the upper end of the canyon like an evil queen on her throne. It's actually a waterfall, a series of pounding stair-step cascades — including one twenty-foot vertical drop.

The vertical drop had me worried the most, but I had a plan. I hoped to nose into the fall, parallel to the banks, and then follow a diagonal angle upward and across the crest of the fall. I hit the bottom of the rapid and started up the right side at 75- to 80-percent power. I crept diagonally up the falls, a foot at a time. When I reached the top, I kept powering it up. Constantly crawling left, I was at about 90 percent power when I reached the left side of the chute — and the boat had no more power to give. It just stayed right there. I knew that if it couldn't give just a bit more, it would fall back down.

The boat, now on full throttle, just hung on the brink. The bow reached just above the falls but couldn't gain an inch. Then, like a teeter-totter in slow motion, the bow eased downward toward the water on top of the falls. An eternity crawled by. Finally the bow touched the flat water above, and the boat wallowed forward. The stern cleared the falls, and the boat leveled off. I made it!

FROM THE BOILING POT I joyously romped the quarter of a mile to our final staging area. The chopper was there and the fuel was there. At 4:25 p.m. I picked up my brother Joe and another helper as crew members for the boat.

We began motoring upstream. Two hours later we went ashore, built a big bonfire, and camped for the night. The next morning we woke up to a blizzard, with blowing snow.

We broke camp and headed up the final 151 miles of river. About three o'clock that afternoon we reached the Paxson Bridge across the Susitna, where we were met by my wife and a couple of our crew people. We pulled the boat out and headed home.

And how did I feel? Exhilarated. Very, very exhilarated. For years I had imagined making this first-ever run up Devils Canyon. And then I went ahead and did it. ∎

A wall of brown fur rippled in the breeze.

9

Saved by a Bear

---

*It was midnight, and a long night of
wind, snow, and cold lay ahead. The
temperature continued to plummet,
threatening the hypothermia that is a
forerunner of death.*

It was to be the bear hunt to end all bear hunts.
The men were going out to seek the trophy of
a lifetime. What they brought back was a rare
story of survival in which the hunted gave life to the
hunter.

T HE BLIZZARD had announced itself with a swelling fury. Swirling wet snow blew horizontally across the land, engulfing everything. But as time passed an eerie silence accompanied the fall of large white flakes.

The brown-bear carcass lay red and lifeless in the grass and willows where the two hunters had left it. It was gradually freezing solid and gathering a blanket of snow.

As the giant bear had fought for his life, so too the hunters now struggled for theirs, just over the ridge from where they had left the carcass. They had finished skinning the bear and started for their camp, only to be halted by darkness and mounting snow. They had built a crude shelter of alder limbs as protection from the wind and snow.

Bob Brister, a hunter from Houston, Texas, and Hap Mathis, his sixty-year-old Alaskan guide, shivered in the blackness, stoking green alders onto a smoldering fire. While waiting for the dawn, they relived the steps that had brought them there, and they wondered if they would survive the storm.

BOB BRISTER remembered the night that Hap's boss, Alaskan hunting guide Ray Loesche, had spun his tale of a monster brown bear. Brister sat in the home of his hunting buddy, architect Kenneth Campbell, and the two avid hunters listened wide-eyed to Loesche's story of an outsized bruin he'd spotted several times from the air.

The huge bear roamed an isolated valley on the Alaska Peninsula, Loesche said. It was a place where no airplane could land, a distant area few would even consider hunting because of the difficult access. This only whetted Brister's imagination. He jumped at the challenge of hunting that bear; it would be the trophy of a lifetime. Brister and Campbell booked with Loesche and flew to Alaska for an October hunt. Campbell would hunt moose; Brister had his sights set on the storied bear.

THE HUNTERS LANDED in Ray Loesche's base camp, a homey place where cabins clustered along the shore of Ugashik Lake. The weather report predicted blowing rain and blizzard conditions. But Brister was anxious to get under way; with each passing day, bears were disappearing into their winter dens. Although Ray Loesche was beginning to have some doubts about the bear hunt, he

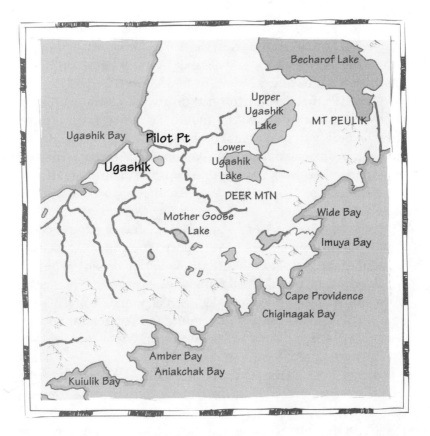

assigned guide Hap Mathis to the enthusiastic Brister. Loesche went with Campbell to stalk a giant bull moose.

Between base camp and bruin lay twenty miles of trackless hills choked with brushy ravines and rolling hummock-dotted tundra. Brister and Mathis loaded their gear — including sleeping bags, food, a pup tent, and some emergency rations — into backpacks and waved goodbye to base camp.

On reaching the hunting area, they stashed their bedrolls and gear along a creek and continued upstream, looking for a better campsite and for sign of bear. The weather was changing, for the worse. A light drizzle turned to snow, pelting the men, who were already wet to the skin. Brister began to question his decision to race a blizzard on foot for a bear pelt.

Suddenly they spotted what appeared to be a large brown bear. But closer inspection with binoculars showed that the sight was actually a recently dug mound of dark brown earth — not a bear but a bear's den.

Brister laughed at the mistake, but Mathis knew they were in danger. No bear wants man near his den. They retreated from the area. When they were at a safe distance from the den, Mathis told Brister how a similar experience had ended in tragedy.

Lloyd "Penny" Pennington had discovered a bear den in the fall of 1955, Mathis related. He invited Everett A. Kendall to go after the bear with him the following spring. The men landed in Pennington's plane and snowshoed almost to the den. They removed their snowshoes and walked up to examine the den — where they were met by a brown bear that attacked and killed them both.

Brister and Mathis sat for half an hour, observing the den and the surrounding countryside. They enjoyed the solitude at the base of Mount Peulik, eighty miles from the village of King Salmon.

They watched and waited but saw no bear. Brister persuaded Mathis to let him inspect the den; Brister wanted to take some photos. They fired a couple of shots into the sky to roust out any bears that might be around and then approached the cave-like den.

Large tracks at the entrance convinced them that the resident was a large boar. It was a typical bear's den, with room for the animal to enter, just enough space inside for him to be comfortable during his winter sleep, and situated so that winter snows would seal the entrance while still allowing in air to breathe. Claw marks indicated a bear had been at work there a short time ago.

After examining the den, the men resumed the search for a campsite. They skirted some alders, then dropped down to the creek and split up. They were looking for a way across the creek, which was too wide to jump.

MOMENTS AFTER they separated, Brister heard a grunt. A wall of brown fur rippled in the breeze a short distance away, above the alders. The bear! In a heartbeat the bear dropped from sight and crashed through the alders.

Brister cleared his rifle and removed the scope covers. Suddenly the bear was moving at express-train speed toward Hap Mathis. Brister squeezed off a round, which echoed simultaneously with a roar from the bear. Brister saw the bear bounce off the ground, roll to its feet, and begin to come for him in giant bounds, pulling the earth to itself. Brister fired again, head on into the bear as it broke brush in its effort to get to him.

The bear rolled, bit at its wound, and was up and coming again. Slamming his last round into the chamber, Brister knew he'd have to make it count at point-blank range.

Ten yards separated man and beast when Brister fired again. He thought the shot was low. But the bear slammed to a stop and slowly sagged to the ground like a collapsing hot-air balloon.

Mathis rushed up. The guide, whose job included protecting his client, explained that he'd been unable to fire for fear of hitting Brister.

The men sat down, shaking from excitement. They decided that the bear had either been stalking them or hiding from them when it began its rush. They approached the bear and examined its wounds. The first two shots had entered a shoulder and the chest; neither would have stopped the bear before it reached Brister. But his third shot had broken the bear's neck.

The huge animal had badly worn teeth with festering cavities and porcupine quills in its tongue and lips. A scar from an old bullet wound traveled across the head and jaw before entering the back; the bullet had obviously missed the spine.

FALLING SNOW and a rising breeze chilled the men. They wanted to remove the bear's hide, but they also needed to return to find their camping gear. Brister volunteered to look for the gear, but Mathis said he needed his help to skin the 1,400-pound animal before the hide froze on him.

Three hours of grueling work later, the hide with skull attached slipped from the bear. It was now dark; they weren't sure whether their gear was upstream or down. Brister began working his way upstream while Mathis held his flashlight as a signal. Brister began falling through the swamp ice and into holes in the tundra, bringing frustration and exhaustion. His search was hampered by falling snow, which was blanketing everything.

A long search along the creek bank showed Brister the futility of finding the gear in the dark. He was heading back to find Mathis when the blizzard struck. He fired off a shot to get the guide's attention. After a long wait, he heard a responding shot. Now in near panic, Brister plunged toward the sound, fighting alders until he saw the beam of the guide's flashlight reflecting off low clouds.

Exhausted, Brister was reunited with Mathis, who was trying to start a fire. He was removing the wet outer layers of bark and wood from alder limbs to get to the dry fibers inside. He heaped a pile of shavings into a cone along with tiny sticks and, with the aid of a candle, lit the wood. Snow hissed at the fledgling fire, threatening to douse it. Soaked to the skin, the men knew that heat and shelter were synonymous with survival. Meticulously they shaved wood and kept up the fire-building process.

Finally a flicker of flame became stronger than the wet, sticky snow. As the tiny sticks heated, they gradually dried the larger ones, coaxing more flame from the wood. It was nearly an hour before any real heat reached the men's hands and gradually began to warm them.

Once they had heat, they sought shelter. It was midnight, and a long night of wind, snow, and cold lay ahead. The temperature continued to plummet, threatening the hypothermia that is a forerunner of death.

They gathered more wood and used it to build a rough lean-to. Now they turned to the bear for help: they spread the bear hide on the ground, fur side up, under protection of the lean-to. They wrapped themselves inside the thick hide beside the fire and waited for daylight. Exhausted, they fell asleep.

Only a short time later they awakened to discover they were encased in a frozen bear hide, trapped in its icy grip. They rocked back and forth, trying to loosen the hide, and were finally able to pry it from themselves.

After the bizarre experience with the bear hide, the men spent the night gathering alder and feeding it to the flames. The snows continued to pile up. The wind picked up, threatening to scatter the fire, and the men tried to block the wind with their bodies. Brister got too close to the blaze and his coat collar caught fire, burning his neck.

MORNING BROUGHT daylight but no end to the snowfall and wind. Two feet of new snow lay on the ground. They must find better shelter.

The bear den.

That was it! They could stay in the bear den until the storm ended. They stashed the bear hide near the fire and marked its location with Brister's orange backpack. Stiffly they trudged up the slope to the vacant bear den.

They entered. The den was as they had left it, damp and

earthy. For the first time since their ordeal began, they were out of the wind.

Mathis chopped wood for a fire. They burned the fire right inside the den, the entrance serving as a chimney. They grew warm and comfortable.

The next urgent need was food. Again the bear came to their aid. Mathis found the bear's carcass nearby and chopped off a chunk of meat, returning with it to the den. He cooked the meat thoroughly to kill any parasites, and then the men ate heartily as the blizzard raged outside their snug cave.

It seemed apparent that the blizzard would last for a few days. By nightfall more snow had accumulated. The men went to sleep, waking periodically to maintain the fire.

They were awakened just before dawn by a smoke-filled den. The wind had shifted. They decided to strike out for base camp, reasoning that they were now rested and that the wind shift indicated a change in the weather. They feared that the longer they waited, the more snow would accumulate, making it even tougher to travel. They retrieved the bear hide and set out to find Ray Loesche's base camp.

The deep, fresh snow was next-to-impossible to walk in without snowshoes. They sank to their knees with each step and often fell through snow-covered bushes and into holes. They crossed ravines and marched over hills, always confronted with more of the same. What kept them going was the knowledge that they wouldn't be safe until they reached camp.

Hours later, exhausted, they topped a knoll and sighted Ugashik Lake and the cluster of cabins dotting its shore — still miles away but a blessed sight. With waning strength they forced themselves to put one foot in front of the other for several more hours to reach the camp, where they were welcomed by Kenneth Campbell, warm cabins, and food. Their bear of a hunt was behind them. ■

We slammed broadside into a mountain.

10

Three Fateful Days

Our main fuel tanks exploded on impact, engulfing the plane in flames. Don was slumped forward, blocking the only door out of the cabin. We had to get out. Our bodies were afire and the wing-tip tanks were still full of fuel.

That day in September 1975, the life of Amelia Hundley shifted into another gear. For the next three days she would experience an amazing ordeal, unexpected and profound. It had started as a one-day round-trip airplane trip from Hoonah to Haines, Alaska, for Pat Sawyer, Don and Evelyn Arbuckle, and Amelia. Here she tells the story of what happened instead.

T O TRULY UNDERSTAND my story, you must know that it is rooted in a uniquely twentieth-century experience of faith. The limits of my Christian being were about to be defined exactly, and I was to discover God waiting for me at the place of my limitations.

It was an unusually beautiful day that early Saturday morning in Game Creek, Alaska, on the northeastern side of Chichagof Island in Southeast Alaska. The island village of Hoonah served us with telephone communications, post office, and landing strip.

It was September 13. A cold wind swept past me as I stood drinking in the unbelievable beauty of God's handiwork, which stretched out in all directions. As I looked across the meadow of mature hay, rippling in the wind, simple thoughts rested pleasantly in my mind: *What beauty! What awesome beauty!*

My eyes feasted on the blue waters of the Pacific, set before a backdrop of pristine forest that covered the mountains beyond. I hadn't the least idea what lay in store for me that very day, nor the adventure that would tax me beyond belief over the next several days.

I had been at Game Creek for about three months. My daughter Wendy had finished high school before we left Charleston, South Carolina, in early June. We joined the first few people who had already arrived, knowing that many more would follow.

Our purpose for migrating from our varied home locations to the wilderness of Southeast Alaska was to establish a Bible center in the context of Christian community. The land that had been purchased for that purpose was located a couple of miles across Icy Straits from the native village of Hoonah.

The residents of Hoonah almost immediately referred to us as The Pilgrims. They said it correctly, for truly we were. Some residents made us feel welcome, but some were strongly opposed to our presence. But none of the pilgrims ever questioned that this was where we belonged. Our ordained direction was sealed upon our hearts, and we determined that this was where we were to be. We were home.

Air or water transportation is the only means of travel between Hoonah and Haines, and many people own small airplanes or boats. When some friends came to visit in two small planes, we seized the opportunity to make a trip to Haines to view some land that had been purchased sight-unseen before leaving Charleston. A second group planned to establish another Bible center there in the spring.

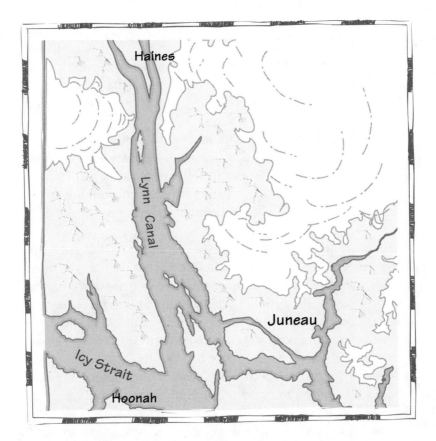

Back at our cooking and eating lean-to, Sam and Lee Fife, Tom Rowe, Don and Evelyn Arbuckle, Pat Sawyer, and some of the other pilgrims enjoyed a hot breakfast of oatmeal, scrapple, and steaming coffee. We laid out our plan for the trip.

We would take both small planes to Juneau and fly from there to Haines to walk the land. We would then fly back to Juneau for fuel and return to the landing strip in Hoonah. We had to be back to our island home before the Alaskan darkness closed in.

Sam would fly his plane, taking his wife Lee, Tom Rowe, and Mike Lopez from our farm. I would fly in a Beechcraft BE 35 Bonanza with Don and Evelyn Arbuckle and Pat Sawyer, our pilot. She was one of our best pilots and the plane was new, so I felt quite safe.

We were excited about our plans as we started the thirty-minute trek across the mud flats to our skiff, which would ferry us down Icy Straits to Hoonah. Half an hour after reaching Hoonah we were airborne.

Great happiness filled my heart as we cruised above the verdant timber and the glacial rivers of the Chilkat Mountain Range. Icy fingers of Pacific Ocean waters poked inland along the coast, and countless tree-studded islands showed their heads above the blue waters. The panhandle of Southeast Alaska runs along the Canadian border, blanketed by sprawling Sitka spruce forests and myriad glaciers, streams, and mountains.

At Juneau we filed our flight plan and took off for Haines. We touched down on the dirt landing strip at Haines around 11:30 a.m. A friend drove us out to the 160-acre parcel, which turned out to be set in majestic mountains with a stream running across the back. I would have a good report to take home with me!

BY 3:30 IN THE AFTERNOON, we were back at the Juneau airstrip. It was overcast, and the forecast indicated possible fog. We filled the main gas tanks and the tip tanks of both planes. We had to fly by sight as there were no radar stations to bring us in by instrument. But we knew that we could fly low and follow the water channels if need be. After some discussion, we decided to go ahead with the twenty-five-minute flight to Hoonah.

We left Juneau at about 4:30. But less than fifteen minutes later, we had reason to regret our decision as we found ourselves engulfed in fog.

The pilot of a small plane must be able to see in order to avoid Alaska's mountain dangers. In fog, a pilot will sometimes choose to stick to his course and count on using charts. At other times the risk is so great that climbing above the peaks proves less dangerous. Sam Fife chose to stay in the fog and follow his instincts.

We heard his quiet voice through the white gloom, over the radio, giving our pilot, Pat, instructions on how to set her course. But when Pat found our plane enveloped in the thick fog, she feared hitting a mountain and climbed out of the fog.

Once our plane was above the mountaintops, Pat encountered a hazard of high-altitude flying in bush planes — the lack of oxygen coupled with the cold. The Bonanza was now above the fog, providing visibility to ensure avoiding the mountains; however, frost began to cover the instrument panel, forcing her to plunge back into the fog.

Visibility was zero. I couldn't even see our wing tips. It seemed like fog was in the plane with us. But it was not fog that was in the plane; it was Someone, and He chose that moment to make

His presence known: "Amelia, you're going to crash." I heard the words clearly. "You won't be killed. You'll suffer for a while, but you'll learn many things as a result of it."

"Lord," I prayed, "I've always wanted to know You as my God. And if this is what You've planned for me, I'm willing. But if I'm not willing, I'm willing to be *made* willing."

I laid my head on the back of the seat and relaxed. When I did, everything in me associated with natural fear disappeared.

MOMENTS LATER we slammed broadside into a mountain in the remote area called Lynn Sisters. It is next to a glacial mountain and is a haven for all kinds of wildlife.

At the moment of impact we had our seat belts on. When the plane stopped, my body kept going. The force of impact stretched my five-foot-two body, tearing muscles and separating bone joints that clicked together as we came to rest.

Our main fuel tanks exploded on impact, engulfing the plane in flames. Don was slumped forward, blocking the only door out of the cabin. We had to get out. Our bodies were afire and the wing-tip tanks were still full of fuel.

"Don! Don! Open the door. Open the door, Don! We're burning!" Those panic-filled words will ever be branded in my mind. Don was too injured to respond to my desperate cries. Behind us the flames tore through the tiny plane. My balaclava, that warm, foldable mask meant as protection from extreme cold, was melting into thick goo and felt hot and sticky under my fingers. I frantically tried to put out the flames that were burning my hair.

I kept calling out to Don to rouse him. I saw flames coming from my hands. At one point I dragged my hands over my face and was shocked to find that my whole face seemed to slip under their touch.

Then Don rallied and got the door open. He lurched and lunged awkwardly out the door and immediately fell away, rolling down a steep embankment.

Evelyn and I were next. We were fortunate to get solid footing, escaping a fall down the mountainside. Once we were safely out, Evelyn said, "Oh, my God! Pat's still in the plane!"

Evelyn climbed back into the plane to get her. Though Pat was nearly incapable of movement, we managed to get her out. Running and stumbling together down the slope, the three of us fled the aircraft, which was burning brightly and threatening to explode again.

At last the four of us came to a stop in the fog between the utter stillness of the mountain and the violent burning of the airplane. The flames on our clothes were now extinguished. The air suddenly rocked with a second and a third explosion, and the rest of the plane burned up.

We had about three hours of daylight left. We didn't know where we were. My face was badly burned.

Evelyn did what she could to make Don comfortable, and I did what I could to help Pat. As night drew near, we settled down to try to sleep. We prepared our minds for what might come next.

I thought of my family and their response to the news of our disappearance. Two of my daughters were waiting for me at Game Creek. I prayed for them and for my friends at Game Creek.

The air was very cold because of the nearby glacier, and I was painfully aware that I was wearing only a cotton jumper with a cotton blouse. As darkness fell, so did the rain, which never completely stopped throughout our ordeal. Our clothing never dried again.

We now faced a new danger, hypothermia — a condition where the body loses more heat than it is able to produce, resulting in the core of the body getting colder and colder until one dies.

THE NEXT MORNING Pat asked Evelyn and me to move her to a more comfortable place if we could. In our earnest attempt to do so, the three of us slid farther down the steep slope. Here we found a wing that a tree had sheared off before the plane hit the mountainside. We dragged the wing to where Pat lay and jammed it between some trees, where it shielded her from the rain. I tucked my shirt over her.

Evelyn and I stayed near the plane so we would be seen if someone spotted the aircraft. By nightfall, search planes did fly over. We found an open space and waved furiously at them. But because we were surrounded by tall, thickly grown trees, we were not seen.

We spent a long Sunday on the mountain, thankful to be alive and expecting to be rescued. As the day wore on, it became clear that Don was failing fast. We began to think we were not going to be found and that we would have to get off the mountain by ourselves.

That night as we tried to sleep, I suddenly thrilled to the sound of footsteps, like the sound of men tramping through the woods. *Rescuers!* I thought. *We've been found!*

Suddenly I realized with concern that the ground shook as the footfalls approached. These were not the footsteps of men. It had to be bears! I recognized the distinct smell of bears drifting through the rain and fog. They were drawing close to us, circling as they approached.

My mind flashed back to a childhood Sunday School lesson in which the Israelites were going into battle with an enemy they could not conquer. God told the king to put praisers and musicians at the head of the army and to advance on the enemy. This so confused the enemy that they fell on one another in their haste to retreat, giving the victory to the Israelites.

So I began to sing and to praise the Lord with all my might, singing loudly into the quivering darkness. Sure enough, the bears ran down the mountain.

We fell into some needed sleep. It was a fitful night of thoughts and awakenings. It was apparent that we could not be seen from the air. We were not going to be found. Our only hope of getting off this mountain alive was by the help of God Himself. I determined that at daylight we would leave the crash site and start trekking down the mountain.

I was intensely aware of the constant rain and cold, but didn't understand at the time how necessary these discomforts were. Our damaged bodies required both the water and the cold. Without the water we would surely have perished of dehydration due to burns; without the cold we would have become badly swollen and lost the use of our muscles.

As DAWN APPROACHED, Don died, leaving three anxious survivors. I removed two pieces of cloth from Don's clothing to use as cushions for my burned hands. We monitored Pat, who was still conscious but incapable of travel. When it was light enough for us to discern shapes, Evelyn and I left Pat and started down.

Before us lay the dangers of further injury, hypothermia, wild animals, cliffs, and waterfalls. Centuries-old fallen trees blocked our progress, and thick branches impaired our visibility. But I had an assurance that we would certainly get out and return home again.

As we began our descent, I grew uneasy. I somehow knew that we would first have to ascend the mountain before we could intelligently descend it. It took several hours, but at last we reached the top of the mountain, where we could see the lay of the land and chart our course.

It was still raining steadily, and we were cold to the bone, but we rejoiced in discovering that we were being led by the Spirit of God. We could see an impassable river below in the direction that we had chosen that morning. Had we not ascended the mountain, we would have spent half the day getting to the river and the other half returning to our poor little camp. We picked out a course for us and, with stiffened muscles and aching joints, started downward.

Not long after, we saw a bear across from us on a knoll. Blueberries were in season, and he was raking through leaves and berries with his paws and shoveling them into his mouth. The bear was huge.

Between us and the bear the ground was covered with deadfalls and boulders. Our chosen path lay through the deadfalls and across the knoll. We made our tedious way over this terrain, and when we reached the other side, the bear was gone.

We continued on, conquering obstacle after obstacle — we crossed gushing mountain streams and detoured around cliffs, brush, and devil's club. We forced ourselves on, pulling off a few blueberries to eat as we went.

We came to a stream, and my intuition told me we needed to cross at the top, where there was a waterfall. After we crossed, we poured the water from our boots, put them back on, and kept going. We walked, and sometimes we crawled. At some places we slid down the mountain on our buttocks. We even slithered on our bellies through some tight spots.

It became too dark to see. Exhausted and still suffering from the rain and cold, we prepared to spend another night on the mountain. It was now about 9:30 p.m. on Monday, September 15.

I WAS TOO COLD to sleep that night, but I remember marveling that both Evelyn and I felt no pain from the crash. Our only suffering came from stiff muscles and from the wet, penetrating cold. We knew that back at Game Creek, our small community would be in constant prayer for us. On the mountain we carried on a compelling prayer life with our Maker.

We rose at daylight on Tuesday and passed another long and arduous day traversing the mountains. As night drew near, we crossed a thick muskeg bog very carefully because we knew there could be sinkholes. We then pushed through dense woods. Suddenly we stepped onto the firm sand of a beach. Looking out over the open water, we saw a boat less than one hundred feet from shore!

The men on board were lowering a skiff over the side. "Yell, Evelyn, yell!" I said. "Yell for all you're worth."

I fashioned a flag by attaching a piece of cloth to a stick. I waved the stick back and forth in the air, yelling all the while. The men heard our cries and came to pick us up.

As I boarded the boat, I told one of our rescuers, "I dreamed last night that two hunters were going to pick us up, but I didn't know they would be two fishermen."

"Lady, we're not fishermen," he said. "We're hunters. We were just fixing to go into those woods to hunt bear. If you had come out of the woods just a little later, we would already have been in there. If you had chosen any different point to come out, we would not have met you."

I was shaking uncontrollably from hypothermia and was in shock. By a stroke of mercy, one of the passengers on the boat was a registered nurse, who gave me emergency treatment.

The captain of the boat radioed the Coast Guard, which dispatched a helicopter to us. Evelyn got on the helicopter to guide the pilot back to our crash site.

One of the hunters wrapped me in his down parka, and his body heat in the parka began to penetrate my body. In an attempt to warm me up, they forced me to eat some hot moose stew. A short time later the helicopter took us to the hospital in Juneau.

The FAA later told us it was unbelievable that we survived the crash. We were told that a plane going at that speed and impacting directly into a mountain should have caused the seat belts to penetrate our bodies, killing us.

In the days after Evelyn pointed out the crash site, several attempts were made to reach it by foot to retrieve the bodies. But no one succeeded in getting to the site.

Finally on the sixth day, the fog lifted and a helicopter recovery team was able to get to the crash site, accomplishing what trained, able-bodied men with equipment couldn't. Pat was where we had left her, under cover of the Bonanza's ruined wing, having passed on to her heavenly home.

Evelyn and I were able to work our way down off the mountain through terrain that turned back the mountain-trained men who tried to get back up to the crash site. They failed to accomplish what two little ladies in their fifties could, through the strength and direction of God. Surely this is His story. ■

The screams turned to gibberish and sobbing.

11

Seventy Feet Below

The screams turned to gibberish and sobbing. Virgil was finally able to make out Scotty's frantic, desperate words: "He's got me! Oh, God, he's got me!"

The legacy of adventure stories from the first half of the twentieth century in Alaska includes some anecdotes of divers encountering octopuses or squid in the waters of the territory. Here is a tale that diver Virgil Buford used to enjoy telling about the old days of Alaskan diving. Buford referred to the creature in this story as an octopus.

A DIVING CREW was on its way to retrieve an anchor that had been separated from a floating fish trap during a storm in Southeast Alaska. The men aboard the vessel heading to the Cape Edgecumbe area were well acquainted with the dangers of their trade. But the weather was good, and they had no reason to expect trouble.

The crew consisted of divers Virgil Buford and Scotty Evans, a big-shouldered Swede (whose name is not known), and a deckhand named Jerry, who knew where the anchor was. All four men knew the anchor was both heavy and valuable. If they could retrieve it, they could split six or seven hundred dollars.

Scotty Evans was in Alaska for the first time. He didn't have his diving suit with him, so he shared Virgil's, and they alternated diving. At the dive site, the Swede manned the air line and Scotty controlled the voice hookup as Virgil dropped overboard.

Virgil understood that the waters off Cape Edgecumbe were infested with octopuses. The sea was open, however, and he felt he was in no danger from the animals.

Virgil slogged along the bottom, encountering a number of octopuses, which fled his presence. Whenever he looked up through the clear water, he saw the shadow of the boat. After two hours with no sign of the anchor, he surfaced to give Scotty a chance.

Scotty's diving experience was limited to areas around docks, and he had never encountered an octopus or squid. He pumped Virgil for information. Virgil told him not to worry; that even if he came upon a large one, it would leave if given a little time to do so. The men fastened a three-quarter-inch lifeline rope to Scotty in addition to the air line, and over the side he went.

Virgil could hear Scotty as he spoke over the voice hookup from the ocean floor. Scotty's voice became animated by surprise and nervousness whenever he saw an octopus. The animals invariably swam quickly away. Scotty settled down to the business at hand, searching for the anchor, and the three men above heard little from him.

Then Scotty said he had discovered a very large octopus in a cave. Scotty told the big Swede to send down a spear if he would like the creature killed for use as halibut bait. The Swede eagerly sent a spear down to the diver.

Scotty, acknowledging receipt of the spear, said in a waiter-

like manner, "One octopus coming up." His comment was followed by silence — and then by a bloodcurdling scream. The air line and the lifeline both jerked spasmodically as the terrified screaming went on and on.

Virgil hollered at Jerry and the Swede to haul Scotty up. They bent to the task, but they couldn't budge the diver, who seemed cemented to the ocean floor.

Virgil asked Scotty what happened. From seventy feet below, all he heard in reply was hysterical screaming.

Virgil tried to calm the diver. He spoke soothingly, repeating the same words again and again: "Scotty. We're trying to help you. What happened? You've got to tell me what happened."

The screams turned to gibberish and sobbing. Virgil was finally able to make out Scotty's frantic, desperate words: "He's got me! Oh, God, he's got me!"

Scotty finally began talking, and a relative calm came over him. He was able to tell his story and to hope for help from above.

Scotty said that when he speared the creature, he had thrust the weapon too low into its body to kill it. The animal instantly shot two tentacles around Scotty's left leg. Scotty pulled out his knife to cut himself free, but he lost it in the struggle. Now he was being pulled from above by his would-be rescuers and from below by his would-be killer.

The solution would have been for a second diver to go below to kill the creature. But Scotty was wearing the team's only diving suit. There was no time to go get another diving suit, even if the men knew where to find one.

While holding tension on Scotty's air and life lines, the men searched their minds for a way to save him. They considered trying to lower the boat's anchor over the animal, following Scotty's directions, and dropping the anchor onto its head to kill it or frighten it away. But both man and beast were under a rock shelf. They considered lowering down another spear, but with Scotty now under the rock shelf, he would be unable to reach it.

Virgil put up a distress flag. The men ran the air and life lines around a cleat, applying as much tension to Scotty's leg as they thought he could stand. They waited and waited.

Half an hour later, Virgil asked Scotty how he was doing.

The weak, almost inaudible reply came topside: "I can't hold out much longer. My leg's numb. What are you going to do?"

Virgil asked how badly the beast had been hit, hoping they could expect it to lose strength and release the diver. Scotty said he had speared it pretty good. Virgil tried to encourage Scotty by telling him that another boat would be along shortly. Scotty said he didn't think another boat would be much help. Virgil just asked him to hang on.

While the men sought a solution, the compressor continued its rhythmic *popa, popa, popa*. The sun shone brightly, and the sea remained calm. Above the surface of the water, all appeared well, with no hint of the drama seventy feet below. One hour dragged into two.

Virgil filled the compressor with gas as the men continued to keep tension on the lines to Scotty, who was becoming frantic. The men on the boat could offer words of encouragement but no action.

At last Scotty broke. "I can't stand it! No boat's coming. They can't do a thing even if one did. I can't stand no more. I'm out of luck."

Virgil responded by accusing Scotty of being a coward who lacked the nerve to tough it out. The verbal abuse got through to the crying diver, who said he could wait a little longer.

A short time later, Scotty offered a calm assessment of his predicament. He said that at first, he thought the creature would tire before long and let him escape. But now he concluded that the animal might hang on to him for days. Scotty said he knew there was a limited amount of gas for the oxygen-producing compressor; once it was gone, so was his air supply, and his life. He asked the crew to power up the boat and pull him away from the death grip.

Virgil was afraid they would pull Scotty's leg off or in some other way severely injure him. Scotty assured Virgil he knew the dangers, but said anything was better than staying down there.

"Start pulling!" Scotty said. "You'll get most of me."

Jerry eased the boat into gear to try gradual pulling. Virgil told Scotty to give him a moment-by-moment account of how it was going as the boat pulled. "Start pulling," Scotty said.

The vessel inched forward. The lifeline tightened.

"How's it going?" Virgil called to Scotty. He got no answer.

The tightened lifeline suddenly became slack and changed from an angular to a vertical position.

"Virg! Virg!" Scotty shouted. "I'm coming up!"

Virgil jumped for the lifeline, yelling simultaneously. Jerry cut the engine. The three men hauled on the line and dragged the diver upward. Scotty broke the surface.

But it wasn't Scotty that the men saw. They saw a giant, pear-shaped creature atop Scotty's helmet, tentacles wrapped around the diver's body. Virgil reacted on instinct. He grabbed a pike pole and thrust it through the head of the beast, and it fell away.

The men brought Scotty aboard, where they removed his helmet and stripped away his suit. Scotty stretched out on deck, shut his eyes, and devoured long-denied drafts of fresh air. The creature had held him on the bottom for three hours.

Scotty had no further desire to look for the lost anchor. He was content to let the octopus clan guard it forever. ■

Pat resolved to continue his journey regardless of the consequences.

12

Left and Lost

A thick fog settled in, bringing dampness and discouragement. During the night he dreamed of hovering helicopters. He awoke to find nothing but his wet jacket and cold body. He wrung the water from the jacket and then tried to go back to sleep during one of the cruelest nights yet.

 Tragedy and near-tragedy in the wilderness can grow out of the simplest misstep or change of circumstance — a single wrong turn, a bit of poor weather. Pat O'Donnell had plenty of time to ponder this lesson during an epic three-week trek for survival.

A S PILOT Francis "Dizzy" Brownfield watched the fog settle in, he admitted to his startled friend Pat O'Donnell that he was lost. He landed the two-place Piper Cub on a gravel bar and rolled to a stop just short of the river, prepared to wait out the weather on this September day in 1949.

As the men dealt with this minor setback to their plans, Pat's wife and another friend were back in the main hunting camp on a river some fifty miles behind Sheep Mountain, which is about 125 miles northeast of Anchorage.

Dizzy's plan for the day was to ferry his pal Pat to a good caribou hunting area, let him take a good bull, and then fly him back to the main camp. But now they were just killing time on the gravel bar. Luckily the fog was just a simple turn of fortune, nothing to worry about.

Dizzy tried to radio Sheep Mountain, but his transmitter was too weak to make contact. As they waited for clearing skies, the men spotted a caribou on the far bank. Pat got off a shot at the bull with his borrowed .30-.40 Winchester, but missed.

Suddenly there were more important things to do. The weather had improved, and the men decided to take off. The plane bounced along the ground in a routine bush takeoff, trying to gain speed. But it hit a puddle, spraying water everywhere and cutting the ground speed.

Dizzy stopped the plane to look for damage and quickly found it. A gaping hole split the tough cloth fabric of the plane's belly, allowing water into the fuselage. They tilted the plane to drain the water and discovered a break inside a wing where the wing tip had hit the ground.

Pat volunteered to stay on the ground. With a lighter plane, Dizzy would have a better chance to hit takeoff speed on the short strip of ground. Dizzy would fly out, patch the plane up a bit, refuel, and be back soon. When he returned, he'd look for a better spot to land.

In the meantime Pat, carrying the rifle, would start for camp on foot (he was pretty sure he knew the right direction) and would also keep an eye out for Dizzy's return.

The damage to the plane meant a tough takeoff; Dizzy barely cleared the end of the short strip. Airborne, he circled Pat, waggled his wings in the bush tradition that says "all's well," and disappeared.

PAT BEGAN A SLOW WALK up the river, scanning every gravel bar along the way for just the right one for Dizzy to use when he flew back. Dizzy wouldn't be gone long. Pat even stopped at one gravel bar and cleared weeds, dirt, and rocks from the site for an airstrip. He gathered enough driftwood for a fire.

Then he sat down for a rest and a smoke. A bush plane came into view. Could it be Dizzy? Pat watched as the plane disappeared beyond the horizon. Four hours had elapsed since Dizzy flew away, and Pat was becoming a little concerned. Using his cigarette lighter, he built a fire.

Now the doubts began to set in.

Could something have happened to Dizzy? And which way should he now travel on foot to find the hunting camp, where his wife waited?

Pat trekked to the top of a nearby mountain, gaining a view of nearly a dozen miles. He spotted a long river bar — a good candidate for a landing strip — and set off for it. He tired, and finally stopped to build a fire before nightfall. He smoked his last cigarette.

Pat spent an uncomfortable night trying to stay warm by feeding the fire between bouts of sleeping, dreaming, and doubting. He awoke to the need for decision: should he stay put or press on? He decided against waiting for an uncertain rescue. His best hope, he felt, was to head west. He struck a westerly course, hiked up a hill — and immediately began doubting his decision to move on. He returned to his fire below.

Vacillating between the fear of leaving his new camp and the need to get on with his own rescue, Pat hiked to the top of the hill and returned several times before spotting a herd of caribou. He had the rifle, eleven shells, and no idea how long he would be on what was suddenly beginning to look like a survival trek.

Pat got off three shots at the caribou and failed to make a hit. The animals moved off a ways, and then they moved back toward Pat. The wind was right and the cover sufficient to permit him to get within thirty yards, where he dropped a bull.

He cut the hindquarters from the carcass and carried them back to his camp, where he stoked the fire and dined on caribou steak. Then he settled down for another long and lonely night by the fire.

The next morning, a distant hope that Dizzy had landed somewhere upstream sent Pat in that direction, toting one of the caribou hindquarters. It began to rain. Pat's feet hurt; he was cold and miserable. His diet for much of the day was wild blueberries.

While surveying a driftwood-covered gravel bar up the river, he heard an airplane. He fired off a round from the rifle, but earned no response. As so many people before him had discovered, the pilot of a plane seldom hears or sees a person down below. The plane's noise is too great, and a man is but a speck in the vast wilderness.

Frustrated and depressed, Pat went through the motions of building a fire to cook a meal. The wind blew as the rain fell. He ate more caribou meat and went to sleep beside the fire.

DAY FOUR. Pat spent the day feeding fires, trying to get warm and dry, and hoping for sight of another aircraft. There was none.

As another cold September night approached, he yearned for a sleeping bag or tent. For clothing, he had underwear, leather boots over wool socks, military fatigues, a field jacket, and a mackinaw. No hat. He had a handkerchief, pocket knife, belt knife, cigarette lighter, and the rifle. That was it. No food except for the caribou meat he had carried and the blueberries that he picked.

He spent another restless night on the ground near the fire, warming first one side then the other and wondering if rescue would come.

DAY FIVE. Clear skies prevailed. But no one had come to his aid, and it seemed that no one would. He resolved to make it out on his own. Cutting the caribou meat into hand-sized pieces, he cooked and ate his fill. He had enough steaks left to provide him with three a day for six days. For some reason, he believed this would be enough time to find help.

It was another day of frustration and disappointment. Trying to cross a rapids, he was tumbled into the cold, slapping water, his rifle banging on the streambed boulders. In the midst of this turmoil he heard another airplane. He escaped from the rapids and fired off a round as the plane disappeared from view.

Later in the day he stumbled onto a lake and discovered human footprints and a tin can that only recently had begun to rust. He shouted in vain. His trek took him next that day onto some ridge tops. Suddenly, another airplane. He stripped off his T-shirt and waved it frantically, with no response from the aircraft.

He encountered moose and caribou and thought about shooting one. But what for? He already had meat and didn't need to pack the additional weight.

That afternoon Pat reached a glacial stream powerful enough to tumble large rocks. He feared crossing, knowing he would be helpless if he broke a leg. He heard more planes, and he settled on a plan. He would build three fires, an international signal of distress.

While gathering firewood, he found signs of former human habitation: a wagon wheel and a lantern. His spirits soared. For the next two days he stoked the signal fires, feeding green wood onto the flames to create smoke.

DAY EIGHT. Pat allowed his fires to die, and with them a little more of his hope for rescue. He moved upstream, searching for a place where he could cross safely and could keep his rifle and cigarette lighter dry. He was almost successful. Just before reaching the opposite bank, he sank into sand and lurched forward onto his hands and knees, jamming both rifle and lighter into the sand.

The rifle was okay, but the indispensable lighter wouldn't light. He cleaned the lighter, using a knife, and remained hopeful that he could get it working again. But that night, the lighter was still out of action, and he endured a cold, fireless night.

The next night was worse. A thick fog settled in, bringing dampness and discouragement. During the night he dreamed of hovering helicopters. He awoke to find nothing but his wet jacket and cold body. He wrung the water from the jacket and then tried to go back to sleep during one of the cruelest nights yet.

DAY TEN. He pressed on with what was becoming an eternal trek. He dropped into a gorge, crossed to its other side, and ascended the adjoining mountain. On the other side of the mountain, another gorge — the deepest yet. With the help of a walking stick Pat worked his way into the gorge, maneuvering around one drop-off after another.

The stream at the bottom of the gorge was like so many he already had crossed: running strong, and pushing boulders before it. He finally crossed safely and got out of the gorge. He began following the bank of a large stream. As Pat rounded one curve, he discovered, to his astonishment, a cabin.

Pat called out. No answer. The cabin door was nailed shut, but next to the door was a hammer. He got the door open and entered the dwelling. Information inside told that the cabin's owner was Oscar Vogel, a longtime guide who operated out of Anchorage. To Pat's joy the cabin contained a stove, bedroll, and grub. His excitement soared with discovery of tobacco and a pipe.

Soon after the coffee was brewing, Pat responded to a noise outside the cabin, thinking that perhaps Vogel had returned. He jerked open the door to find two grizzly bears staring him in the face. He slammed the door and clambered onto the bed. But the bears were not interested in Pat or his brew and departed while he stood on the bed, rifle in hand.

Life was looking so much better. He had food. The cabin provided comfort beyond belief. He decided to stay for a couple of days to recuperate.

DAY THIRTEEN. Pat awoke to find his feet feeling better than they had for some time. Before setting off downstream, he filled a jar with cooked beans and borrowed a piece of tarp, a wool blanket, and a pair of rubber-bottomed boot pacs. He left his worn-out boots behind.

By the end of the afternoon Pat came across another of Vogel's cabins. It was larger than the first and appeared to be the base of Vogel's operations.

The next day Pat helped himself to matches and candles before continuing downstream. That evening Pat discovered yet another of Vogel's cabins, this one on the opposite side of a stream. When he had difficulty crossing the water barrier, he realized how weak he was getting.

The cabin didn't have much in the way of food, but Pat exchanged a pair of dry wool socks for his worn-out ones on the morning of his fifteenth day alone in the wilderness. Pat spent the next four days crossing streams and mountains. He nursed his way along on throbbing, badly battered feet.

DAY NINETEEN. Late in the afternoon it began raining. He became discouraged and was again without food. Then Pat discovered another cabin. Inside were eggs, bacon, potatoes, flour, butter, coffee, and sugar. He prepared a feast and then went to sleep in the warm, dry cabin while rain pounded the roof.

DAY TWENTY. More rain. But Pat was determined to continue on his way. Hardly had he started when he fell into a stream and drenched himself. He decided to return to the cabin, dry out, and spend another night, enjoying the roof's rainy lullaby.

Several airplanes flew over the area that afternoon, and that evening he spotted a beacon light some five or ten miles away. With renewed enthusiasm he saturated an old blanket with kerosene in preparation for building three signal fires.

The next four days, however, brought only rain. Pat tried to cross the stream in front of the cabin but kept falling into the water. He feared being swept downstream and drowned. Fog shrouded the cabin. Even if someone had been flying, he would have been hard-pressed to detect Pat. He stuck tight to the cabin.

DAY TWENTY-FOUR. Pat resolved to continue his journey regardless of the consequences. He made pancakes for the trail and left the cabin. At the stream, he again fell in the water. But on the third try, he made it across.

The next stream crossing was deep and narrow, so he tried to jump across. Landing on the far bank, he clung to a branch with one hand and draped a leg around a tree as he tried to edge out of the water. He finally succeeded in pulling his wool blanket and rifle from the water and easing up the bank to safety.

Four hours farther downstream Pat heard a light airplane take off. In his excitement he fired a round from his rifle. He moved on and within five minutes heard a dog bark. He shouted jubilantly to the dog. He continued yelling every thirty yards. Minutes later he began hearing the sound of chickens.

And then he heard a man's voice. They yelled to each other a few times before Pat looked across a stream and could see the man. Pat waded his final stream and stepped to safety. He was on the Alaska Railroad, only a mile from the rail-stop community of Talkeetna, a hundred miles north of Anchorage.

AFTER PAT WAS REUNITED with his wife, he began to put together the pieces of all that had happened in the past twenty-four days. He figured that he had covered more than 200 miles in his trek from the gravel bar, where he landed with Dizzy, to the village of Talkeetna.

When Pat and Dizzy failed to return to the hunting camp, Pat's wife and their other hunting partner managed to walk out to the Glenn Highway.

Three days later and fifty miles north of the hunting camp, the 10th Air Rescue paratroopers found Dizzy's airplane where it had landed safely on the side of a mountain. It had a flat tire and was out of fuel. The paratroopers found signs of Dizzy's attempt to hike to safety, but he was never found. ■

A gust picked up the plane and slammed it toward the bay.

13

The Sand, the Wind, and the Waves

I prayed that this was only a nightmare.

Clyde M. Dahle left Togiak, Alaska, in his single-engine Taylorcraft airplane at 11 a.m. on Sunday, October 16, 1983. His destination, Hagemeister Island, lay only twelve miles away. He was going beachcombing. He was well-equipped with survival gear — but he was not prepared for the events that would test his faith in himself, his fellow man, and his God.

I DROPPED IN LOW over the beach on my final approach and caught a close-up glimpse of the landscape, dominated by sand and waves. The touchdown was pretty good, considering the crosswind, and it wasn't too tough to skirt the basketball-size rocks. My mind was partly on the fun in store after I landed. *Wonder what I'll find today? Maybe some glass balls.*

The wind was gusting to twenty-five miles an hour, but it wasn't anything I hadn't dealt with before. Actually the weather was pretty normal for this part of Alaska, which is 400 miles southwest of my home in Anchorage. The temperature was a little warmer than usual, about thirty-five to forty-five degrees Fahrenheit.

I was taxiing toward a stop when suddenly a gust picked the plane up and slammed it toward the bay. I remember thinking, *This can't be happening. I've got to get it faced into the wind.* But it was too late. The wind brought the wing up and I was airborne. My power was at idle, and there was no way to get enough power for takeoff. In two seconds I was in the water off the island's steep cliffs.

My first thought was, *I'm gonna lose my plane. I've worked too hard for this.* But as it started sinking, ice-cold seawater rushing in from all sides, I told myself, *I've got to get out of here. Got to keep a cool head; don't panic.*

I unhooked the seat belt and took the emergency locator transmitter — the ELT — out of its rack behind the seat. I had to move fast. The water was already over my head. I grabbed my bag of survival gear and started to move to the door.

But I couldn't budge. No wonder. I forgot to get out of my new shoulder harness. I longed to push up toward any air that might have been trapped at the top of the cabin, but I was harnessed in and couldn't move. I felt caught in a water-filled coffin.

I got the harness buckle free, and I floated upward inside the cabin. The door was now below me. I had to get down to the door or I was finished. I worked the door, and it opened. I swam out, the ELT in my left hand and the drawstring of the survival-gear bag clenched between my teeth. I was now out of the plane, but still underwater and beneath the wing.

I pushed free of the final obstacle, the wing, and burst to the surface to gulp air. But I lost hold of the bag, and with it went my survival gear: matches, lighters, sleeping bag, rain gear, tent, food, flares, smoke signals, and mirrors. That wasn't my most urgent

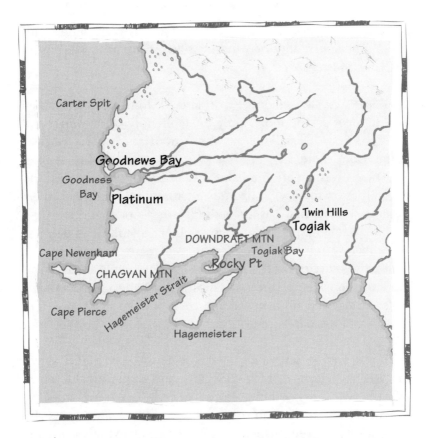

concern, however. I was at least fifty feet from the beach, with the wind and waves pushing me and the plane farther from shore. I knew I couldn't survive more than a few minutes in the frigid water. I had to get to shore.

First I tried swimming on my back. I'm a strong swimmer, but I didn't make much progress. I tried it on my stomach, with a swimmer's stroke. I was tiring, and I wasn't helped by all my heavy winter clothes: wool underwear and socks, denim pants, chamois cotton shirt, fiber-filled parka, cotton gloves, wool hat, rubber insulated boot pacs. I tried to swim harder, but my feet keep going down. I was exhausted. *My God,* I thought, *I'm not going to make it. God, don't let me die after all this.*

I kicked onto my back again to force my feet up. I was beyond exhaustion, but I was determined to keep trying. I was not going to give up.

And then a wave pushed me onto the beach. I held on, afraid I'd be washed out again. And then I could only lie there. I couldn't move. I was cold, wet, exhausted. My hat was gone, along with one of my gloves, and the wind blew across my bare, wet head. I lost consciousness.

WHEN I REVIVED, I could see my plane, floating about a hundred and fifty feet off the shore. Only the white tops of the wings and the tail surface were visible as the current and wind pushed it farther from shore.

There I was, on an uninhabited island, with only my ELT and the clothes on my back. I had no way to dry my clothes or to get warm in weather that was just above freezing. And with the setting sun, the temperature would drop another ten to fifteen degrees.

Shivering terribly, I barely managed to stand. I must have pulled the muscles on the insides of my legs while I was swimming to shore; the pain was excruciating. I had to get out of the wind. I staggered up a hill at the edge of the spit of land and squeezed into a narrow crevice between rocks — and blacked out again.

It was raining when I regained consciousness. I shuffled down the beach, in front of high clay cliffs, and found a place where over the years the pounding waves had carved a cavern out of the bank. I crawled inside and collapsed on the cold, damp ground. I was shaking uncontrollably, a definite sign of hypothermia, the cooling of the body's core that leads to death. The shaking got worse. I couldn't get my breath, and my heartbeat was going crazy. I passed out.

When I awoke this time, it was late afternoon. I removed my clothes long enough to wring the water out. I found that I still had my two pocket knives, including the Swiss army knife with several blades.

With the screwdriver blade, I opened the case of the ELT. I blew out the water and tested the instrument. No luck. I would get no quick rescue, because the ELT was unable to send the signal that could be picked up by a satellite or airplane.

Exhausted from working to get back into my wet clothes, I lay down in the cave and fell asleep. When I awoke, it was dark, and I could see nothing. I heard the surf slamming on the beach and the rain falling. I was shaking so uncontrollably that I kept banging my head on the roof of the cave. The hole was only big enough to permit me to lie flat; it was about six feet long, three feet wide, and two feet high. I had to move to the cave's entrance to have enough room to turn over. I couldn't lie on my back because of the pain in my legs.

I was extremely thirsty. I found a small stone in my coat pocket and put it under my tongue and sucked on it. I could still taste the seawater in my mouth.

Again I fell into an exhausted sleep. I was afraid I would not awaken again. I believed that I would just shiver and shake until all my energy was gone and then die in my sleep. I thought of my family, my wife and five children. I wondered how they would be able to go on without me. I prayed that this was only a nightmare and that I would wake up in the morning to find the airplane tied down on the beach.

AFTER WHAT SEEMED like an endless night, I woke up on the morning of Monday, October 17, to a cold day with a high overcast sky. The wind had subsided, and the rain had stopped. I felt lucky to be alive — until I tried to crawl out of my hole. Everything hurt!

I sat for a long time at the entrance to the cave. I looked at the ELT. I tried to blow the circuitry dry with my breath, but the seawater had corroded the works. Discouraged, I laid it aside. I thought my chances of rescue without the ELT were not good.

I tried to think of something positive. I would have been reported overdue by this time, and both my family and those back in Togiak knew where I had gone. It would be only a matter of time until they would be out searching for me. *I must keep myself alive until they get here,* I told myself.

I struggled to my feet and limped down the beach to the spit. The airplane was no longer in sight, and all I found was the sand, the wind, and the waves. *It's as though nothing has happened,* I thought.

With the heel of my boot I scratched out an SOS in letters twenty feet high, in the sand above the high tide line.

The next mission was to find drinking water. I walked the beach, still sucking on the pebble. I found a stream in a ravine where I could get out of the wind. I drank my fill and carried some water back up the ravine in a glass jar I had found on the beach.

I took off most of my clothes and hung them on bushes to

dry. It felt good getting them off. I wrung the water out of my wool socks and felt insoles. I cut some long grass on the hill above the beach, intending to use it in the cave to insulate the ground if I had to spend another night.

LATER THAT DAY I spotted my first aircraft since I fell into the sea. I recognized it as a Search and Rescue plane because of my years as a pilot on search missions for the Civil Air Patrol. It was an Air Force HC-130, and it flew over the island at an altitude of about two thousand feet. I stood at the top of the hill, frantically waving my white undershirt. The crew didn't see me waving and didn't spot my SOS in the sand.

The plane will come back, I thought. But it didn't. The plane, now just a black dot, slowly turned and disappeared.

Then I realized the crew was trying to spot my airplane. An all-white plane in this country sticks out like a sore thumb. But my plane was gone, taken by the sea. I knew that the crew would never see me unless I made myself more visible.

I began hauling white, basketball-size stones from the beach up to the black sand on top of the spit to outline my SOS letters and make them easier to see. Carrying the rocks was painful and tiring, and I needed frequent rests. I found a white garbage bag on the beach and tied it to a long stick as a flag. I waited until dark, but no other aircraft came. I was not discouraged. *I will be found tomorrow,* I thought.

As the temperature dropped below freezing, I walked back to the cave to prepare for another miserable night. I noticed that parts of the cliff above the cavern had sloughed off during the previous rainy night — and I realized there was a chance the whole thing could break loose and bury me in my cave. But I felt I had no choice for a shelter, and I again climbed into the hole.

A red fox came down the beach and walked up to the mouth of the cave, stopping about ten feet away. "Looking for a meal?" I asked. He jumped back, startled.

I shivered myself to sleep in clothes that were still damp. Waking off and on during the night, I prayed for warmth, good weather, rescue — and cliffs that would not come down on top of me.

The only things keeping me even remotely warm were the wool thermal underwear, wool socks, and insulated rubber boots. Even though the socks and boots were wet, they kept my feet from becoming frostbitten. I kept my one remaining glove on one hand, and I put the other hand in my pocket to keep my fingers from frostbite. I wrapped my head in my undershirt as a makeshift cap.

AT DAYLIGHT the next morning, the fox was back, this time with a friend. *They're like vultures*, I thought, *but they haven't got me yet*. I crawled out of the cave and tried to stand but couldn't. I was weak from a night of shaking and shivering and trying to keep warm. I hurt everywhere. I sat for a long time, pondering what to do next.

Before the accident I had flown over a fish camp a dozen miles away, across a river on the far end of the island. I wondered if I could walk to it. I decided to stay where I was and to build a bigger sign for searchers. I would also cut more grass for my cave and concentrate on conserving energy to keep warm.

Struggling to my feet, I staggered out onto the spit, carrying the white garbage-bag flag. Now I began hauling white rocks from the beach. On a patch of black sand on top of the spit, I scratched out another SOS — this time with letters more than forty feet high. I outlined the letters with the white rocks. The work kept my body warm and my mind occupied, but it required frequent rests and trips to the stream for water.

I harvested more long beach grass, thinking I might be able to burn it if only I could get a fire started. There was no wood to burn; the island was covered only with tundra.

I found an old tracked vehicle on the beach, nearly rusted away. Scattered around the vehicle were a foam-rubber seat cushion, a couple cans of oil, a partially filled can of WD-40 lubricant, some boards, and an old pair of wool gloves. I carried these items back to my cave.

With renewed hope I took the ELT apart and sprayed the circuitry with WD-40. I took the battery out in hopes it could make a spark and start a fire, but the idea didn't work. I cut up the foam-rubber cushion for insulation from the ground and for a pillow. I kept busy the entire day doing things to improve my chances of being found, carrying my white flag with me wherever I went.

Toward dark on Tuesday, I realized that not a single plane had come over all day. *The weather is good enough for flying*, I thought, *but maybe they can't get out here. They must be looking in the wrong place, maybe on the other side of the island. They'll be back over here again. They won't give up after searching this area only one time.*

I thought of my wife and children. *They haven't given up on me. They will see me through this with their faith and prayers.*

Just before dark, I heard the unmistakable sound of a light single-engine aircraft. I stood on the beach and frantically waved my flag as a small, dark-colored aircraft appeared in the distance. It flew over the middle of the island and disappeared high over the hills.

I sat down on the beach and shivered until well after dark. I felt that I had done everything I could; that my rescue was now out of my hands. Totally dejected, I dragged myself back to the cave. Even with all my improvements, the cave was cold and lonely.

The temperature that night, my third holed up in the cave, was down to about twenty. I had taken my wet boots off and packed them with dry grass. I wrapped my feet in grass to warm them up, but I woke numerous times during the night, shivering and shaking, my feet freezing. I tried to wrap them in more grass, but it didn't help. I put the wet boots back on. My feet never did get warm. I prayed they would not get frostbitten.

AFTER WHAT SEEMED like endless darkness, the sun rose. I was so stiff that all I could do was sit at the cave entrance and look out to sea. It began to snow. I turned and looked toward the mountains, now covered with snow. *Please, Lord,* I prayed, *don't let it snow and cover up my signals.*

It was Wednesday morning. I had been hanging on for four days with nothing to eat, and I was burning up energy trying to keep warm. I didn't know how much longer I could last.

The day brought some new discoveries. On the tundra above the beach, I located a little something to eat: half a handful of lingonberries. I also found a rusty quarter, a can of charcoal lighter fluid, and an old .22-caliber shell. I took a ball of cotton that I was carrying as tinder and tried to get the ELT battery to strike a spark to ignite it. It didn't work. I broke open the .22 shell and dumped the powder onto the cotton and pounded on the primer of the .22 shell to try to set it off. This didn't work either, although the powder appeared dry.

Out at sea, a storm was heading my way. It was snowing again in the mountains and over the sea south of me. I was becoming very discouraged, and my stomach ached with hunger.

About noon I spotted a large multiengine aircraft across the strait, fifteen miles away. The airplane turned and headed toward me, slowly, ever so slowly. It was flying less than a thousand feet above the water and heading right toward me.

It can't miss me, it can't miss me, I kept saying to myself as I ran down the spit toward the plane, waving my white flag.

I stopped running when I got to the middle of my large SOS and stood waving the flag in a big arc over my head. *Let them see me,* I prayed, as the airplane came closer and closer. It was a Coast Guard Hercules HC-130, painted a beautiful red, white, and blue.

The plane passed over and then turned and headed back out over Bristol Bay. It went maybe ten miles, but then made a wide circle and came back toward me. *They've seen me!* I thought. I knew it was true when the pilot turned on the plane's landing lights as it passed over me a second time.

SUDDENLY I WAS no longer weary; I was flying high. I was as high as that pilot who right then was saying on his radio that I have been found and will need to be picked up. Another HC-130 quickly showed up, this one from the Air Force.

I walked back to my cave and looked at the odds and ends I had accumulated. I picked up the rusty quarter. *My good luck piece,* I thought as I put it into my pocket. I picked up my ELT and walked back out onto the spit. I started to erase the SOS markings I had made and began scattering the white rocks. I wouldn't have been seen without them and without the large white garbage bag as a flag.

The Coast Guard HC-130 dropped a large can on a parachute. It contained a radio and a box lunch. I immediately ate a candy bar and then used the radio to identify myself.

Within minutes an amphibious Cessna 185 landed in the ocean and pulled up to the spit. The co-pilot came over to me.

"Boy, I'm glad to see you guys!" I said.

"It's good to see you alive too," he said. "Mike will hold the airplane while we get aboard, and then we'll take you back to Dillingham."

"Sounds great to me!"

Once the plane was airborne, I felt safe and warm. I looked out the window, down at the scene of my mishap. There was no sign I had ever been there. All I could see was the sand and the waves. ■

Her pulse quickened, and her eyelids fluttered.

14

Precious Cargo

Now the trapper faced the dismal task of dealing with the body of the Eskimo, which had frozen solid.

 Tales of survival often take unexpected twists and turns. One of the most unusual is this story from nineteenth-century Alaska.

O N THE DAY that trapper James Holveg found the Eskimo's
body, he had risen early at his cabin in Chignik on the Alaska
Peninsula. The yellow rays of an oil lamp provided light for dress-
ing and for cooking breakfast. He fed his big malamutes their daily
meat ration and got them ready for the push thirty-six miles inland to his cabin at Black Lake to retrieve his cache of furs.

A violent storm had swept the country for the past twenty-
four hours, blanketing it under new powdered crystal. He knew
that in the coming weeks, spring thaws would fill the wilderness
streams.

In the crimson moments when the sun touched the mountain peaks in the early-morning chill, Holveg kicked off on his
dogsled. His many days of winter trapping alone were about to
pay off. It had been a good season, and the winter catch awaited
him at the Black Lake cabin.

But then he came across the other dogsled. Lying beside it
was the body of a man. Holveg could only guess at the hardships
the Eskimo had faced in his final hours on earth. How many snow-
covered miles had he pressed his team of dogs, with wolves shad-
owing his trail? One of his final acts had been to cut the traces of
the dog harness to free his animals, giving them a fighting chance
against the cunning killers of the great white silence.

The year was 1897, in the month of March. The Eskimo was
unknown to Holveg, who now stood over the body.

HOLVEG'S DISCOVERY of the Eskimo brought back troubled memo-
ries of an earlier tragic incident. One day, when Holveg was new
to the territory, he had heard two rifle shots ring out as he traveled along a lake. After a long interval he heard a third and final
shot. Thinking nothing of it, he continued on his way.

The following spring, while dogsledding on the opposite side
of the same lake, Holveg made a ghastly discovery. In the area
from which the three rifle shots had come was a human skeleton. The rusty jaws of a huge bear trap clasped the skeleton's
crushed leg bone; a rifle lay nearby. Through the skull was a single
bullet hole.

NOW HOLVEG faced the dismal task of dealing with the body of
the Eskimo, which had frozen solid. The dead man would have to
be transported to Chignik. Holveg first checked the contents of

the sled. It was loaded with furs. Holveg was amazed at both the quantity of furs and their quality; they were worth a small fortune.

He lifted one fur after another, working his way through the fox, lynx, mink, and wolf hides toward the bottom. Only then did he receive his greatest surprise.

At the bottom of the load, loosely covered with fine fox skins, was a young Eskimo girl. Her face was uncovered. He peeled off his mitts and touched her skin; she was pale and cold but alive. He loosened the parka that framed her face, lifted her from the sled, and laid her on the snow. He guessed her age to be twelve or thirteen, and he marveled at her beauty.

Holveg moved her arms and legs and slapped her face to stimulate circulation. Remembering he had a jug of sourdough hooch, he hurried to his sled. He returned with the jug, parted the girl's lips, and poured some liquor into her mouth. Her pulse quickened, and her eyelids fluttered. She would make it.

Holveg's immediate goal was to hasten the girl to the nearest village for medical treatment. He emptied his sled, placed the girl in the sled along with the Eskimo's furs, and sped to the closest hamlet. He knew an American couple there who could help with her.

Holveg sold the furs of the dead Eskimo and he sold his own. He used much of the fur money to care for the girl. The next year, she left for Tacoma, Washington, where she lived with family friends of Holveg and attended school for five years. At the end of her schooling, during her eighteenth year, Kueuit returned to Chignik.

It was then that she married her rugged rescuer. ∎

The chop in the water increased to powerful whitecaps.

15

Twenty-nine Hours

---

*Hank's situation was growing hopeless,
his battle becoming much more than a
simple physical struggle. Now he had to
also fight the notion of giving up.*

Caught up in the joy of life and the freedom of his work, fisherman Henry Elmore cruised along in his boat at eleven knots, its top speed. The fishing boat was his home and his life, offering him the smell and taste of the sea and the opportunity to sail its waters anywhere, almost any time. On this summer day, he was about to be given the sea's most unforgiving test.

H ENRY ELMORE scanned his fishing grounds from the deck of the *Silent Hank*. July 6, 1952, was not so different from all the many other summer days when he had left Snug Harbor aboard his gillnetter to seek the silver-sided salmon that crowded the waters of Cook Inlet in southcentral Alaska. Blue sky smiled above azure seas.

He skirted the southern tip of Chisik Island, pointing the bow of his thirty-four-foot fishing boat toward the mouth of the Kasilof River, several miles northeast across the inlet. Rumor said the waters were socked tight with sockeye salmon. Silent Hank slipped through a fog bank.

The name of the boat acknowledged Hank's handicap. As a six-year-old, he was accidentally dropped by his mother as she fled a tornado for the safety of the storm cellar on their Oklahoma farm. The accident left Hank unable to speak or hear — a deaf mute. But he compensated for his loss with a zest for life and a love for the freedom he found in Alaska.

The hard-working life of a fisherman had sculpted Hank into a fat-free, brawny young man. His Irish, Danish, and Cherokee heritage and his 210-pound frame made him fit to meet nature and all its demands.

Hank suddenly slammed into the pilothouse as the boat struck something below the surface. He regained his feet. Groggy from the collision, he rushed forward to inspect the damage. He leaned over the side and saw splintered hull planks below the waterline. The boat was rapidly taking on water.

He quickly decided what to do. He would return to port, running in reverse to reduce the water pressure on the bow. And he would plug the hole with a mattress or bedding.

Just as he reached the hatch leading to the engine room, a yellow wall of flame exploded in his face, catapulting him into the water. His heavy clothing pulled him down. He kicked free of his boots and pushed to the surface. With his knife, he cut away his clothing until all that remained were his shorts and the inflatable life belt he wore while fishing.

The boat was aflame, spewing smoke before quickly and quietly dropping below the surface. Hank treaded water, away from the suction of the sinking boat. He looked for some floating object for support, but there was none.

Many boats plied the inlet and one would surely spot him,

Hank thought. He noticed three fishing boats a half dozen miles to the north, with the peaks of Kalgin Island looming up beyond. Someone has probably already seen the plume of smoke and is steaming to my aid, he thought. Rescue is just a matter of time.

It was 9:30 a.m., and he was more than twenty miles from land. How long could his body withstand the thirty-six-degree-Fahrenheit water temperatures before hypothermia set in? He had been told a person's normal body functions shut down within minutes in this water — and that you can't expect to survive for as long as an hour.

HANK SWAM toward Snug Harbor. He picked out a mountain peak and focused his course by it. He wouldn't be able to swim to shore, but he hoped the swimming motion would help circulate his blood and warm his body until help arrived. With calm confidence in his swimming prowess, he started a breaststroke with a frog kick, a motion that he felt would save energy. The life belt resulted both in drag on his progress and in buoyancy.

Steadily stroking toward shore, Hank periodically surged out of the water partway to scan the horizon for boats. At one point he was excited to see a boat approaching. But after several minutes with no telltale vibrations in the water, he knew there was no boat. He discovered he had seen not a boat, but a deceptive mass of floating debris.

He soon realized he was the plaything of the mammoth Cook Inlet tides that flow at speeds up to eight knots. The inlet, eighty-five miles long and up to thirty miles wide, generates tides greater than thirty feet. Hank, caught up in the outgoing tide, was being sucked out to the Pacific Ocean.

He first swam against the current, but soon realized he was wasting his energy. He kept moving toward shore.

More than an hour had passed. Despite the stories of quick death in the waters of the inlet, he was still afloat. The summer sun had apparently warmed the surface of the water enough to let him live. The life belt kept him afloat and near the surface.

Off and on during the day, vibrations in the water told Hank that a boat was not far away. He saw several vessels: commercial fishing boats owned by individuals and also the larger fish tenders that retrieve salmon from the fishing boats. But not one vessel came close enough to see Hank or to hear him.

His situation was growing hopeless, his battle becoming much more than a simple physical struggle. Now he had to also fight the notion of giving up. But he persuaded himself to keep going. To swim was to stay alive.

The rays of the sun burned painfully into his eyes and his face. From time to time he escaped from the sun by swimming with his head beneath the surface, holding his breath as long as possible. He yearned for sundown and a release from the burning pain, but he knew that nightfall would bring colder water and new agony.

He swam, his effort still strong, his stroke slow and rhythmic. He directed his mind away from his predicament and even began thinking about the enjoyment he would find in building a new boat.

The tide changed, and now Hank was being swept back up the inlet. He meditated on the new boat, building it in his mind, board by board. He visualized the keel, ribs, planking, deck, wheelhouse, and power plant. While the boat took shape in his mind, the sun slowly slanted westward into a hazy cloud.

WITH THE SETTING SUN, the water temperature dropped. When Hank paused to rest, his legs sank lower than usual, into the deeper and colder water. He knew he must keep his body as close to the surface as possible.

Hank now tried floating on his back, resting the muscles of his arms, shoulders, and legs. He readjusted the life belt and struck a balance of weight between his lower and upper body. He folded his arms and floated on his back until it got so cold he had to move to warm up. He kept repeating this process.

A wind moved up the inlet about 8 p.m., bringing rain clouds. The wind created a chop in the water and the clouds released rain. By ten o'clock the chop had increased to powerful whitecaps, and Hank was assaulted by stinging spray, making breathing difficult. He also ingested saltwater, constricting his throat. He relieved his thirst by opening his mouth to the rain.

The cold intensified, numbing Hank to the core as the waves pummeled him and disrupted his swimming rhythm. He resolved to put every effort into continuing his rhythmic strokes. The coastline was obliterated by clouds and chilling spray, but Hank used his knowledge of wind and currents to keep heading toward shore.

The physical struggle and the mental anguish continued. During those dark moments, Hank felt his subconscious take over, egging him on to take just one more swimming stroke, then just one more, then just one more. It was as if a power outside himself had taken over. He mechanically took one stroke; he followed that with another and then another. Through the darkness of the night, he kept reaching for land.

HE SWAM THROUGH the night. He was exhausted, but with the dawn he began to feel warmer. He kicked onto his back and rested his weary arms on his chest.

The coastline was now visible, encouraging Hank once more. As birds flew over, gawking and squawking, Hank gave himself a pep talk about life and about his new boat, and he pressed on for shore.

His face was battered from exposure to the sun and the salt spray; his eyes were swollen almost shut. The skin under his rubber life belt had been rubbed raw. But his hopes soared. He was now close enough to the shore to see individual trees.

Just then, another setback as the cold again sapped his strength and brought a lethargy he had not known before. An overwhelming desire for sleep overcame him, and he swam with his eyes fully closed. Consciousness left him, and his body jackknifed, head and legs touching beneath the surface. A strange warmth seemed to envelop him. Moments passed before he suddenly woke up and realized his danger. His mind reprimanded his body, ordering it to stay awake and to keep swimming.

Automatically his body responded, and he resumed kicking and stroking. Almost before he knew it, he saw a shed. Forcing this hallucination from his mind, he kept on. Then he stopped and forced his eyes open with his fingers.

It was really a shed! The shed was a trap house, part of the offshore fish trap south of Chisik Island. Determined to reach the trap house safely, he continued to control his rhythm, swimming with a slow, methodical stroke.

Then he saw a man walk from the trap house. Never had silent Hank yearned so much to have his voice back. He made as much noise as possible by splashing to attract the attention of the trap tender. The man spotted him and rushed to fetch his companion from the house. They launched a skiff and rowed out to Hank.

The men grabbed Hank under his arms and hauled him into the boat. Hank was flooded with the warmth and security of rescue, of human hands supporting him, of the solid feel of the boat's planking. Realizing he was safe, Hank passed out.

It was 2:30 p.m. Hank had been in the water for twenty-nine hours and had traveled more than twenty miles.

One of the rescuers called Anchorage by radiophone. An airplane quickly arrived, took Hank aboard, and returned to Anchorage. Hank regained consciousness in a hospital room. His great stamina and physical conditioning were heralded as his salvation.

Four days later he was back following his dream of freedom — working as a fisherman and making plans for building his new fishing boat. ■

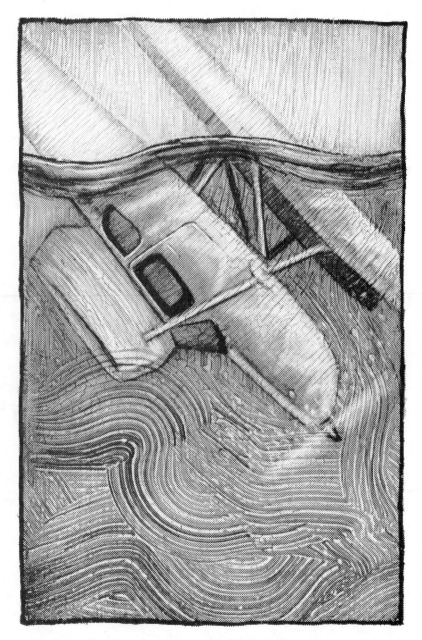

The plane plummeted into the water.

16

He Drew Me Out of Deep Waters

We sank swiftly. Even though I was able to fill my lungs with air, my mouth filled with water. I knew I was going to die.

 The weather was overcast and unusually warm for late September. A steady cross-wind accompanied by gusting winds met the Cessna 185 floatplane as it bounced over the whitecapped waves of Thomas Bay and took off. Suddenly a gust hit the craft with enough power to force it back onto the water's surface fifteen feet below. Sonie Blackwell tells the rest of the story:

MY HUSBAND, GARY, and his hunting partner Mike Woodworth had planned a goat hunt for September 1992. I love the challenge of the woods, hunting and fishing, so I was excited about going along.

We left our home in Juneau with great expectations of a much-needed break. We feel our children are our most valuable resource, so we spend a great deal of time with them. We home-school them. This in itself is a big responsibility, and the financial burden on a one-income family is awesome. We decided a week in the woods would reduce the pressure, provide an exciting escape, and give us an opportunity to obtain meat for our table.

The hunting trip also seemed like the perfect opportunity for me to get away from everyday life and have time to reconnect with my Bible and the Lord. Sometimes it seems that God is so far away. For the last few months the distance between God and me had seemed to grow, mostly due to the pressures of having only a single income and of home schooling. It seemed my prayers weren't being answered. I had no idea at the start of the trip just how much I would be reconnected with God.

The hunt was planned for Thomas Bay, about fifteen miles north of Petersburg in southeast Alaska. From Petersburg, we ran Mike's sixteen-foot Pacific Mariner skiff, with its fifty-five-horse Evinrude, across Frederick Sound and into Thomas Bay. It was September 26.

So there we were on Thomas Bay, in a cabin, ready to relax, hunt, and enjoy. The weather was pretty fair, though a slight drizzle fell. We hit the hay right after a nice dinner so that we could rise early to climb up into goat country. During the night my back began to ache, and I didn't sleep well.

The next morning we cooked a hearty meal: sausage, eggs, and potatoes with onions. The plan was to climb to an elevation of 3,300 feet, shoot a goat or two, spend the night, and return the next day.

Mike grabbed his bow and arrows while Gary shouldered his 7 mm rifle. The pain in my back wasn't getting any better. I knew the grueling terrain was infested with spiny devil's club up to timberline, and I felt my condition would hinder the hunt. So I chose to remain behind. Gary kissed me goodbye and I wished them luck as they departed at 9 a.m.

ALONE AT THE CABIN, I daydreamed that maybe I could shoot a black bear and have the bearskin rug I'd always dreamed about. *While the men are on the mountain,* I thought to myself, *I'll get a bear and have the hide hanging in the tree beside the cabin when they return. They'll be impressed with my great hunting abilities.*

First I took a nap. When I awoke, I was feeling better — and I decided that halibut fishing made more sense than bear hunting. I gathered up my gear — a rod and reel, herring for bait, a harpoon, my float coat, and binoculars — and headed for the skiff.

I motored half a mile out onto the blue, glassy waters of the bay and dropped my line. Although the weather was beautifully sunny, the air was slightly chilly because of the three glaciers that surround the bay. I thanked the Lord for allowing me to live in such a beautiful place.

After four hours without so much as a nibble, I decided my books would be more exciting than the skiff. Off to the cabin I went. I built a fire in the wood stove to take the chill off the air. Then I found a good Christian novel and curled up on the bed.

My back began hurting a little worse, closer to my kidneys. I made a bowl of soup and took some Advil. I could hear the wind, and large drops of rain pelted the roof. I slept fitfully that night and awaited the fellas' radio call the next morning.

The weather was gray and wet. I made a warm fire and lay around the cabin until midafternoon, when the guys called on the VHF handheld radio. They said they would hike down to a point on shore, where I could pick them up in the skiff.

Knowing hunters, I figured they'd be an hour and a half later than the pickup time they gave me. I waited a couple of hours, then headed for the pickup point.

The men were there with one goat. I listened to their story as we returned to the cabin without a hitch.

My pain increased. We assumed it was kidney problems, but I wasn't too concerned. I was moving no faster than a sea slug, but nonetheless I believed I was okay.

Gary and Mike disagreed with me. In spite of my protests, they said I needed to see a doctor. (They didn't want a repeat of the year before, when I fell and cut my knee to the bone during an outdoors trip. I had insisted then that I was fine and walked ten miles, resulting in blood poisoning.)

They called Pacific Wing in Petersburg for a medivac, a medical evacuation. Pilot Dave Reimer planned to pick me up around 12:30 p.m. on the following day.

THE FLOATPLANE LANDED and taxied to the beach in irregular winds. I climbed aboard and strapped myself in for what I thought would be a bumpy ride. Dave closed the door and started the engine. He adjusted the shoulder harness on my seat belt and then piloted the plane swiftly across the water, and we lifted off.

Fifteen feet up, a wind gust shoved us back down onto the water. The plane still seemed to be riding fine, so he throttled it up and we lifted off again.

Thirty feet above the water, the wind hit us again, slamming the plane down. The left wing sliced into the water. The wing ripped halfway up the leading edge to the strut. The plane plummeted forward and the floats were ripped from the fuselage, though they remained connected by some rigging cable. The propeller cut off the front two feet of the right float, flipping the plane over onto its top and spinning it to the right. The force ripped the right wing off and shattered the passenger windows.

We sank swiftly. Even though I was able to fill my lungs with air, my mouth filled with water. I knew I was going to die. I heard the sound of glass breaking. I undid my seat belt and moved forward, managing to get into a small air pocket. I saw Dave undoing his seat belt.

In the air pocket we were still able to talk. I told Dave to open the door. He asked if my seat belt was off. I told him it was and again asked him to open the door. He tried the door and it wouldn't budge. In desperation I said, "In the name of Jesus, open the door."

Just then the door made a popping sound and opened. We were freed, and we kicked to the surface and up to the floats. As we emerged from the water, I said to Dave, "If you don't believe, now is a good time to start."

Dave got up onto one float. I was in the water between the floats, struggling to get onto one. I was hindered by the weight of my wet clothes and by a rigging cable wrapped around my leg. I managed to get free of the cable, and with Dave's help I climbed onto the pontoon.

From shore Gary and Mike had watched the Cessna trying to take off. It was obvious that our plane was being buffeted by the wind. Gary had seen thousands of plane landings and takeoffs, and he felt this wasn't an unusual takeoff considering the weather. But then the wind shear hit.

Instantly Gary and Mike cut the skiff's anchor rope and jumped aboard. On their handheld radio they called the Coast Guard, squawking a mayday. Mike started the outboard and aimed the boat toward our plane.

When Gary and Mike arrived in the skiff seven or eight minutes after we went down, they saw we were all right. Gary hugged me and helped me aboard the skiff. My leg was sideways and Gary thought it was broken. He yelled, "Your leg!" I just looked at him and said, "It's fine."

ON SHORE, Gary helped me change into dry clothes. He kept saying, "Sonie, you're all right. You're all right." We both thanked the Lord for His faithfulness. Then he wrapped me in a sleeping bag and went back to tow the plane.

I stood on the beach in dry clothes, the sleeping bag wrapped around me, silently thanking God and making plans to amend broken relationships. As God had saved me from eternal death eight years prior, He had snatched me from a physical death in the bay. There was no way out of that plane but in the name of Jesus.

I watched the men out in the skiff as they tied onto the pontoons, getting ready to tow the plane. But they had to give up as the floats filled with water and were no longer able to hold the plane on the surface. It sank in 150 feet of water.

Back in the cabin, which was warm with heat from the wood stove, I made hot tea and chicken noodle soup for everyone. While we waited for the *Southeast*, a sixty-six-foot commercial fishing boat, to come from Petersburg to pick us up, we rolled sleeping bags, packed boxes, and restocked the cabin's wood supply. We returned aboard the *Southeast* to Petersburg, where family and friends were told of the plane crash and the miraculous results.

Doctors in Petersburg said my back pain was most likely caused by gall stones. Otherwise I had only minor bumps and bruises. After a physical examination I was released from the hospital.

MOOSE SEASON began the next day, so we went back to the cabin to try to get in some hunting. When we arrived, I became tired and shaky, feeling the effects of all the excitement of the past few days. I went to bed in the cabin and fell asleep.

The next day, divers aboard a 100-foot vessel came into Thomas Bay and secured lines to the sunken plane. They hoisted it out of the icy water. The windshield was still intact. The only item they could not recover was the pilot's door — the hinges were untouched and undamaged, yet the door was gone! God works in mysterious ways.

With shaking hands I removed my wet and swollen Bible from the cockpit and opened it. I thought about Psalms 18:16: "He reached down from on high and took hold of me; he drew me out of deep waters." ■

A wall of water tossed the raft end over end.

17

At the River's Mercy

I heard a crack and felt a rumble. The iceberg began to list, and I adjusted my weight accordingly, desperate to prevent it from rolling. Standing against the current, my iceberg was beginning to fall apart.

Tall tales abound on the last frontier — fish grow in size at nearly every fisherman's telling, weather worsens every time a pilot relates a harrowing experience. But nearly all Alaska tales have at their heart the immensity and grandeur of a land that, even unembellished, still sounds fantastic. This story of the Copper River, completely true, is so wild it borders on the unbelievable. In the pages that follow, Kevin Smith tells his own story.

T HE COPPER RIVER has historically presented a challenge to Alaskans. It was a primary obstacle to railway pioneers and miners at the turn of the century. Nearly nine decades later, this same river challenged my good friend Blake Call to plan a float trip on its waters. I joined him in 1987, along with his parents and two other friends. It was to be a casual six-day float downstream from Chitina for about 100 miles through some of the most spectacular Alaskan wilderness.

Let me tell you a bit about myself and the other folks on the trip. At six-foot-two and 215 pounds, I'm larger than most of my friends. I was raised as an active outdoorsman and have been in Alaska since the pipeline days in the mid-1970s. I didn't work on the oil pipeline, though; I was only twelve when construction got under way in 1974.

I met my rafting partners when I was attending the University of Alaska Fairbanks. Kurt Wold and Blake Call both were close to my age. Shelly Call, Blake's mother, is a whitewater canoe instructor in Fairbanks. David Call, Blake's father, is also a river-running veteran. Both had run the Copper River before. Barbara Cotting was a friend of David and Shelly and, like me, had done some rafting and canoeing but had never faced water the size of the Copper River.

The six of us slipped our two rafts into the Copper River at Chitina at mid-morning on a Wednesday. The trip had barely begun when we spotted the largest bull moose I have ever seen in my years in Alaska. Continuing through Wood Canyon and beyond, we became the audience for a symphony of wildlife and scenic splendor. Trumpeter swans, grizzly bears, bald eagles, and more gave a private performance for the six of us floating lazily by.

We floated, rowed, camped, and ate. The weather was fine — in fact, too fine. The sun, beating down on nearby glaciers, weakened a glacier dam. Late Thursday, the dam of snow and ice burst, sending a surge of pent-up water into the Copper River. The rise in the water level was slow, but the effect was dramatic.

We met the water almost a day later at legendary Abercrombie Rapids. At the rapids, this flowing giant of a river crams all its force into a gorge that is no wider than a few hundred feet. The rapids consist of large oceanlike swells bordered on one side by a house-size rock and on the other by small standing waves. This day, however, only the very top of

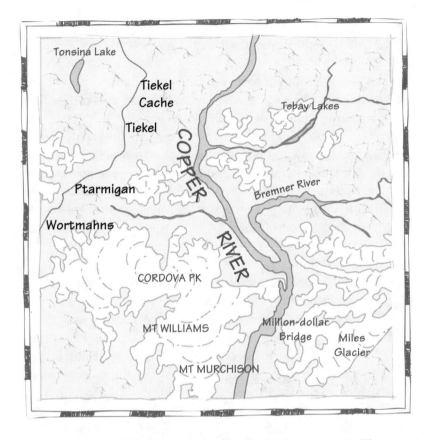

the rock was visible as water repeatedly broke across it. The rapids were a mass of swarming, standing waves whose size we couldn't determine from a distance.

We surveyed the rapids as we approached and agreed to go in, but we still couldn't figure out how big the waves were. I knew that bushes on the side of a mountain that appear to be only knee high can, upon closer scrutiny, prove to be twelve-foot-high alders.

So it was with the waves at Abercrombie Rapids. My estimate, before entering the rapids, was that the waves were cresting at about the height of my thigh. But as we hit the first wave, my error became frighteningly obvious.

We never got beyond the second wave. A wall of water that dwarfed our sixteen-foot raft tossed it end over end without hesitation.

Shelly was trapped beneath the raft, hanging onto the rowing frame, with her head in the airspace created by the foot compartment. David, the helmsman, managed to hold on to the lifeline.

I was not so fortunate. My 215-pound frame was catapulted out of the raft and into the current, and I was swept away.

As KEVIN SMITH fought to stay above water, Blake Call's raft was trailing behind. Blake's raft, with him at the oars, also carried Kurt and Barbara. They were seventy-five yards behind the lead raft, and they had watched carefully as that raft entered the rapids. When the lead raft closely approache d the first wave, Blake was stunned. The water was enormous. The standing waves were twenty feet high.

The lead raft crashed over the first wave and landed, bottom flat, on the uphill surge of the second wave. There it seemed to hover, on a mountain of water, before it was tossed end over end, dumping his parents into the frothing torrent and launching his friend Kevin through the air.

"Row for your life!" Blake shouted, and they did. "They've flipped!" he screamed. "They've goddam flipped!"

They rowed wildly away from the most intense part of the rapids, skirting the waves as best they could on the right. As they rowed away from the main current, the overturned raft moved away from them. Once around the most dangerous part of the rapids, Blake, Kurt, and Barbara rowed with what strength they had left into the current to catch up with the overturned raft. Waves bounced up and down, obscuring their view of the capsized boat. Could the others live through this?

As they approached the other raft, only David could be seen clinging to the lifeline.

"I think I see your dad," Kurt reported. Then the head of Shelly Call appeared beside her husband's as he helped her out from beneath the upside-down boat.

But there was no sign of Kevin Smith.

Through the enormous waves, they finally reached the overturned boat and pulled David and Shelly into the raft. The sound of the river around them was deafening.

"Where's Smith?" Blake yelled.

"The last I saw him, he was floating high," Shelly shouted back. Supported by his life vest, Kevin was last seen being swept to the river's left.

They lashed the capsized raft to the side and rowed into an eerily calm eddy, a kind of whirlpool. It reminded Barbara of the eye of a hurricane. Still the river roared, and the force of the water was so strong just behind the flat spot that the river flowed crazily uphill. The group paused only briefly to make certain everything was secure before trying to enter the raging current again.

But they couldn't break the grip of the eddy. The raft slipped downhill and swirled to the back of the whirlpool. Again the crew paddled madly at the water, trying to reach the outside of the whirlpool, but again failed. Shifting positions for optimum efficiency, and powered on adrenaline, they tried again. This time the raft train broke loose from the eddy and was once again at the mercy of the fast-moving water. Still there was no sign of Kevin.

I MUST GET TO THE RAFT, I told myself as I fought against the current, but it was wasted effort. I was in the river and the river was in control. My paddle — the last vestige of a raft I had already lost sight of — floated toward me, and I grabbed it. This was to be my security blanket for the ordeal that followed.

The water was so big that I felt that I must ride as high as possible. Afraid that the water and silt would fill my rubber boots and hold me down, I kicked them off. As I crested the next wave I surveyed my situation, then took a deep breath and held it as I plunged twenty feet down to the trough and rode back up the next wave for some more of the same treatment. Breathe and survey. Hold on for dear life and plunge.

Fortunately I was dressed as well as I could be for the rapids. I wore wool long underwear beneath my wool pants. I wore a T-shirt, a long-sleeved shirt, and a wool sweater beneath my Woolrich jacket. Wool gloves, wool socks, and a life vest finished my outfit. But even though I may have been wearing a family of sheep, the frigid water of the glacier-fed river penetrated my every pore and set my teeth to chattering.

After riding to the top of several waves, I could understand what awaited me downriver. Below me and to my right was an island flanked on the right side by a line of hungry-looking rocks. If I was to make it to safety, I needed to get well beyond the jagged teeth of the rocks and into the eddy in front of the island. Not a foot less would do, or the current would drag me across the teeth, chewing me up and spitting me out on the other side.

I paddled for all I was worth, but I wasn't doing much good. I picked a spot on the other bank, off to my left, and began to paddle and pray.

I was swept safely past the rocks and continued to paddle toward the other shore, alternately praying and singing "Going to the chapel, gonna get married," a promise I had made to myself and my fiancee of two weeks. Already the frigid water was cooling my body core and hypothermia was setting in; I could hear my voice slurred and thick. I could not feel my feet.

I reached the point where I had hoped to paddle ashore, but I drifted past, unable to get there. I stuck the paddle under my knees, pulled myself into a cannonball, and let the river carry me where it wished.

Thoughts flooded my mind as I realized that I was dying. My life didn't flash before my eyes. It was more a reflective review on what I had done, whom I had loved, and what my purpose in life had been.

I don't hate anyone, I told myself. *This is good. I hold no grudges. I have not seriously wronged anybody. I am doing what I love to do, and I am paying a price that comes with that.*

I thought too of what was supposed to be. Former daydreams of my future swept through my mind. As any bachelor might, I began the trip wondering if getting married was something I was ready to do. Now, floating in the river and about to die, I knew that getting married was exactly what I wanted to do.

I looked around. *This country is beautiful,* I thought. *It truly has the fingerprints of God all over it. If now is the time that I must go, then nowhere could be a more fitting place.*

All the rationalization in the world, however, could not erase one nagging thought: *While I am prepared to die, I am not yet ready to die.*

MEANWHILE, the five other members of the expedition rode the current around the island and pulled in behind it, onto the main shore. As they pulled toward shore, they spotted one of the rubber boots Kevin had worn, swirling in a whirlpool behind the island. Everyone saw the boot, but no one called attention to it. Each chose to file the sight silently away rather than alarm the others. But the seed of doubt about the chances for Kevin's survival was beginning to grow.

Blake and Kurt set off with binoculars to look for Kevin; one walked upstream, the other downstream. It was now forty-five minutes since the raft had thrown Kevin into the river.

As Blake searched, he spotted a dot in the water. He drew his binoculars to his eyes expectantly and focused — but it was only a seal. Again and again this happened, and each time his frustration grew.

Kurt also scanned for signs of life. He spotted movement on the far shore and checked through his binoculars. He saw a huge brown bear tossing and shaking something in the air. He closed his eyes and could only hope he had not found Kevin.

OF COURSE I prayed. I prayed to God to forgive my indiscretions. I prayed for strength to survive.

A seal popped up beside me in the river. This animal with dark, mysterious eyes seemed to know instinctively that I was out of place and in trouble. Curious, the animal floated near me, examining me in his element the way I have examined seals in a zoo. He moved closer, with what seemed like a sense of compassion. It was entirely plausible in my mind that the seal could help me.

Becoming seriously hypothermic, I felt I was about to black out. I drifted in and out of thought. I fought the urge to close my eyes and sleep. My vision got darker and darker, like backing into a long tunnel and seeing the light at the entrance getting smaller and smaller. The light became just a flicker, a point, while darkness surrounded me. My eyes closed — and I bumped into the bottom of the river.

I bounded upward and discovered that I could stand. The water was only about a foot deep. Facing upstream, and shaking uncontrollably from the cold, I planted my paddle in front of me and surveyed the situation. The river was very wide. On either side of my shallow stance, it was at least half a mile to shore. My guess was that I had floated more than three miles down the river.

The warm air felt good. From the position of the sun, I guessed it to be about 6 p.m. I realized I should be dead by now. Since I wasn't, and I was standing on the bottom, things were looking fairly good. The seal surfaced near me again, and I made an appeal for help. It looked at me quizzically and slowly sank into the river.

After about twenty minutes I was warm enough to remove my hood and to shout weakly for help. Weakly, indeed. I was startled at how insignificant my cries sounded in the middle of this muddy giant of a river. Upstream I saw no one. I realized it would be up to me to save my own life.

I tried to move laterally across the river toward the right bank. I knew the chances of finding only foot-deep water all the way to shore were remote at best. Within five or six steps, I was in chest-deep water and the current was forcing me backward. I tried to return to the shallows but couldn't regain the ground I had lost. I managed to get back to water that reached only to the middle of my stomach.

Once again I was shuddering uncontrollably. I planted the paddle in the riverbed and let go to zip my coat up further and replace my hood, knowing I would probably lose the paddle — my security blanket — and too cold to care. I had just taken two steps toward the other bank when the freezing, muddy water sucked me up and once more carried me away.

UPSTREAM, the five rafters had decided on a rescue plan. Blake, Kurt, and Barbara would remain in the area where they were. They would search the side of the river they were on from the rapids downstream and then move to the other side of the river and do the same. Nearly two hours after the accident, it seemed clear that if they were to find Kevin, he would have to be on shore. Staying alive in the frigid waters of the Copper River for more than forty-five minutes was a near impossibility. Chances were slim that a live person would be found very far downriver.

The plan called for Shelly and David to take the other raft and head down the river, keeping a watch out for Kevin as they floated down to the Million Dollar Bridge. At the bridge, a popular summertime tourist spot and the first possible point of human contact, they could try to find help.

Before splitting into two parties, they divided up the gear and food. Very little was lost in the upset because most of the gear was lashed down in watertight bags. Only a few items fell victim to the river: some tent poles, the propane tank for the camp stove, perhaps a case of beer.

They agreed on a system of fire signals. If David and Shelly spotted Kevin but were unable to get to him, they would light one fire at 10 p.m. If they actually picked Kevin up, they would light two fires at ten o'clock. If there was no Kevin, there would be no fire.

David and Shelly pushed off in their blue raft at 6:30 p.m.

BACK IN THE CURRENT, I once again needed to conserve body heat. This time, however, I had no paddle to help me in keeping my knees to my chest, and I was too weak to do so without an aid. I grabbed a piece of driftwood floating by. I stuck the driftwood under my knees and used it to help pull myself into a cannonball.

I bobbed along in the current with the other flotsam picked up by the new high water of the Copper. The seal floated next to me and dived. I prayed again.

I looked up anxiously as I approached the looming Miles Glacier, which was calving off big chunks of ice into the river — loudly and often and in the direction that I was being carried.

My vision was again waning. Stronger than ever was that familiar desire to close my eyes — to succumb to the darkness and let go of the little point of light at the end of the tunnel that was my consciousness and my life. Now severely hypothermic, I was slow in my thinking when I thought at all. My sole task was to keep my eyes open.

As I approached the glacier, icebergs entered the mainstream, joining me and the high-water driftwood in the fastest part of the river. The approach of the first iceberg gave me an idea. I swam awkwardly to meet the ice.

The first iceberg was the size of a coffee table. I reached out with my last remaining strength over the top of the ice, pulling myself near. As I attempted to mount the iceberg, it slowly rolled over and floated bottom-side up. The bottom was smooth and clear from melting in the water and was even harder to try to climb up on. So I rolled the iceberg back over and carefully pulled myself up onto its surface, spreading my weight as evenly as possible across the berg.

Exhausted, I lay on the iceberg, shivering, feeling even colder than when I was in the water. I could feel the heat being sucked from my body like power from a battery.

Towering above me, the snout of Miles Glacier calved again and sent a large wave my way. The wave rolled slowly over the river toward me, closer and closer. It hit me gently and spilled me back into the river, rolling my little iceberg back upside down. I climbed on again, but each time the glacier calved, it sent waves that tipped me into the icy water. This happened four or five times. Each time, it became more difficult for me to swim back to the iceberg and climb aboard.

We continued to approach the glacier, my iceberg and I, closing in and passing other icebergs. I spotted a larger, more spacious, and more stable iceberg. I rolled off my little piece of ice and breaststroked toward the larger, slower-moving berg. This iceberg was big enough, about the size of a large desk, to permit me to get completely out of the water. Cold as it was, it was a definite upgrade.

Reaching from the iceberg, I pulled up pieces of driftwood to put underneath me, to insulate myself from the cold: a piece of wood for a seat, sticks for a floor, and a couple of extras just in case. I was completely out of the water for the first time since I was thrown from the raft, and I was alive!

DAVID AND SHELLY floated down the river. Binoculars in hand and shouting Kevin's name, they drifted and they rowed, scanning both shorelines. They had already come four miles and nearly as many hours from Abercrombie Rapids, and they knew that the fate of their friend Kevin was all but sealed. They discussed the impossibility of Kevin's survival and the possibilities of what would happen to his body. Still they held to a ray of hope and continued to search in the remaining light.

The three people upstream spent the evening until nearly dark searching the shore for Kevin. Disheartened, they silently packed their raft and rowed to the island, each immersed in private grief. Blake, Kurt, and Barbara set up a makeshift camp and checked frequently for signal fires from downstream. Each time they checked and saw nothing, their spirits dropped lower.

WELL, THIS IS GREAT, I thought, as visions of riding an iceberg heroically to safety filled my head. I would simply jump off at the nearest shore as I floated by. Better yet, I could ride the berg to the Million Dollar Bridge and step off, bowing to the tourists. I was alive, getting warmer, and floating toward civilization. Things were definitely looking brighter.

At that moment, the iceberg ground to a halt on the bottom of the river. The silt of the river assaulted the iceberg, sandblasting away at it. I could hear the sound of the sand as it scoured by, and I knew I was in trouble.

Now in Miles Lake, only 400 yards from Miles Glacier, I sized up my predicament. The glacier rose out of the water on my left as I faced the downstream shore a mile or more away. That was the closest shore. Across the lake, the other shore was at least two miles away. Upstream, only 100 yards away, was a sandbar. But with this current, I knew that having the sandbar 100 yards up-stream or 100 miles upstream was pretty much the same: it would be impossible for me to get to it.

I heard a crack, felt a rumble, and out of the water next to me shot two pieces of ice about a foot and a half in diameter. The iceberg began to list, and I adjusted my weight accordingly, des-perate to prevent it from rolling. Standing against the current, my iceberg was beginning to fall apart.

I began looking at nearby stationary icebergs that were more stable, icebergs that were at least the size of a small house. One of these would have to be my next destination. The possibility of spending the night on an iceberg became a very real one.

It was now about 8:30 p.m. The sun was low and a ray of sunlight spread from the distant shore across the lake and onto the Miles icefield in a narrow beam. I sat and pondered my fate. I prayed — and I heard a voice.

Unsure, I removed my hood and looked around. I shouted "Hello" and listened. I thought I heard a shout from the far shore, and I turned just in time to see a flash of blue pass through the narrow beam of waning sunlight. Blue was the color of the over-turned raft.

DAVID AND SHELLY'S raft drifted silently across Miles Lake. Could it be possible? Had they heard a voice? Or was it just an echo from their last cry?

Shelly yelled "Hello." The reply came back, "Hello." It was just an echo; it must have been. The lake was bordered on three sides by glaciers and high mountains, a perfect echo chamber.

Shelly called again. "Hello" she shouted. "Hello" came the reply. "Hello" she screamed. "Hi" came the answer. David and Shelly looked at each other in disbelief.

Then they heard the distant voice again. "Hello . . . hello . . . hello . . . " followed by a message that they couldn't make out, a message overpowered by echoes, distance, and the river. It had to be Kevin, but how, and where? The voice sounded as if it might be coming from the far side of the lake, about three miles away. But there was no shore there, only the vertical face of Miles Gla-cier rising out of the water. Where else could it be coming from?

They finally decided the voice must be coming from across the lake, glacier or not. They paddled toward the glacier.

HAPPY IN A WAY that I cannot describe, so incredibly happy to be alive and to see rescue coming, I forgot entirely about being cold. Adrenaline pumped through my system as I saw the blue dot get larger and larger. I danced on my iceberg island, waving my arms and shouting to my rescuers: "I'm over by the glacier on an iceberg, and my iceberg is melting!"

I continued to shout to help David and Shelly find me in the fading light. I sang "Row, row, row your boat," the echoes helping with the rounds. I told them how happy I was. I also tried to explain that the iceberg I was on was deteriorating and likely to go at any time.

As the raft drew within a mile, they spotted me. Waving back, Shelly yelled, "We see you. Save your energy."

"I don't think you understand," I shouted back. "I'm on an iceberg, and my iceberg is breaking up!" They didn't understand. They thought I was on a sandbar or something. The idea I could be standing on an iceberg never entered their minds.

When they were within half a mile of me, they suddenly figured out the situation. Once they understood, they rowed faster.

About forty-five minutes after I first spotted the raft, it pulled up to my iceberg.

"So that's Abercrombie Rapids!" I said. "What a wild ride!"

"We've never been so happy to see anyone in all our lives!" came the reply.

Then I felt a rumbling under my feet. Now an experienced iceberg pilot, I knew this was the moment. I yelled, "It's breaking up!" And with that I lunged into the air toward the raft.

As I did so, the iceberg I was standing on broke apart, with a sound like a rifle shot. With a couple of oar strokes, the raft was on me, and David and Shelly pulled me into the boat.

Unbelieving, they looked at me. "You're one tough son of a bitch," David said.

"You're right," I replied.

Shelly helped me while David rowed toward shore.

"How do you feel?" she asked.

"I'm afraid I may lose my feet," I said. Shelly put dry socks on me and stuck my feet between her legs as we traded accounts of what had happened since four that afternoon.

It took nearly an hour and a half to reach the closest shore, a sandbar at the base of a steep mountain. I stripped immediately and climbed inside two sleeping bags. David scrambled to find enough wood to light two signal fires. It was well past ten, the prearranged signal time.

Not enough fuel lay on the sandbar to make the fires very large, and it was too dark to collect more wood. But what David's signal fires lacked in communications ability, they more than made up for in warmth. Wearing socks and a sweatsuit and draped with a sleeping bag, I huddled near a fire while a tent was assembled. I tried to eat but couldn't, and I settled for the comfort of the fire.

Later, in the tent, lying between Shelly and David inside two zipped-together sleeping bags, I felt the warmth of their bodies flow into me like I had felt the ice suck it from me. Within ten minutes, Shelly was shivering from having gone to bed with an ice cube. But all of us were exhausted, and we quickly fell asleep.

Sleep didn't last long. Our sandbar was only fifteen feet wide, and the water continued to rise. About three in the morning we awoke to the sounds of water lapping at the tent. For one groggy moment I feared I was still in the river. We quickly pulled the tent as far as we could up the sandbar, tied the raft securely, and went back to sleep.

UPSTREAM, the three other rafters continued to look in vain for some signal from David and Shelly. The next morning, at first light, they moved to the other side of the river and chose a site suitable for landing a helicopter. Then they began the search for Kevin again.

Blake hiked upstream to the rapids and started working his way back. Kurt hiked downstream but soon hit a tributary that blocked his progress. Looking across a long, desertlike sandbar, he could see for miles, and nowhere was there a sign of Kevin. Barbara remained at camp and built a fire as a signal for an eventual helicopter.

Kurt and Blake returned to camp at noon, exhausted and depressed. Without enthusiasm they went through the motions of eating. They tested the helicopter signal fire, sending a billowing smoke signal into the noontime sky. Twenty hours had passed since the raft overturned. Still, each tried to keep the others' spirits up.

Just before the weary band turned in for a midday nap, Blake prophesied, "At two o'clock Smith will come around that corner and say hello."

"HELLO!" BOOMED a voice that woke all three members of the upstream search party. Kurt, Barbara, and Blake stumbled out of their tents, squinting their eyes in the afternoon light. It was two o'clock.

Then they heard another shout.

"Hello the camp!"

Scanning the horizon over the scrub brush and the sandbar, they spotted Blake's mom, Shelly, dwarfed by the owner of the voice, none other than the missing Kevin Smith!

Kurt, Barbara, and Blake ran toward the tributary that earlier had blocked Kurt's progress. Blake led the way, flipping handstands and jumping up and down.

"Smith, are we glad to see you!" they hollered. Shouting from across the stream at each other, the two groups agreed on a time when Blake and Kurt would bring their raft to the tributary. Kevin and Shelly would first go back and get David, who was downstream at Miles Lake with the raft.

IT WAS ONE OF the happiest moments I'll likely ever be a part of, that moment when all six of us were reunited. We feasted and drank, shared our thoughts and fears and experiences, and celebrated life until late into the night.

The next morning, we had a visitor for breakfast. A tiny little sparrow, usually a spooky bird, landed near the campfire and begged for crumbs. Within minutes the tiny bird was flitting from person to person, sharing breakfast with each of us.

As we packed the raft with all the gear, making room for the three extra passengers, Bird remained. Jokingly we referred to the bird as my guardian angel. Jokingly, I say, but I still wonder.

Much of the trip still remained ahead of us. We recovered the second raft. We still had two days of travel before we were to reach our takeout, including floating by the enormous face of Childs Glacier, right next to the Million Dollar Bridge.

This glacier is truly spectacular, but a bit dangerous. The glacier has been known to calve pieces of ice large enough to send a wall of water up over the ten-foot bank on the other side of the river and claim vehicles parked near the shore. We hoped to merely glide past the glacier. As we began to do so, Bird fluttered to our raft and sat on the oarsman's head, undeniably a good omen.

Although the glacier did calve, the wave was small. It missed our raft entirely and merely pushed the other raft to shore, where David, Shelly, and Barbara easily shoved it off again. Bird remained with us for the rest of the trip. ∎

My hands groped helplessly in the darkening gray water.

18

Take Too Long and Die

The sudden force pitched the stern over the bow. I leaped for the side. The boat cupped over me like the closing of a coffin. It went down quickly and silently, taking me with it.

The work of commercial fishermen who operate set nets in Cook Inlet is hard but routine: Set the nets, check the tides, pick the fish out of the nets, get the fish to market. But July 18, 1990, turned out to be far from routine for Jim Aronow, an Anchorage teacher working for the summer on the crew of fisherman Lance Hughes. The temperature hovered at forty-five degrees at the fish site five miles northwest of Kenai. Aronow, forty-two, powerfully built at five-foot-nine and 175 pounds, needed all his strength to survive the ordeal he describes here.

S ALMON RUN in seasons and they run in schools. They don't arrive singly or five at a time; they arrive five thousand, ten thousand, or twenty thousand at a time. When the fishing's hot, it's not uncommon for our nets to fill immediately. Then we pick the nets clean so more salmon can run into them.

When the fish are thick, we start at one end of the net and drag it up and over the skiff, picking the fish and letting them fall into the bottom of the boat as we allow the empty net to slide back into the water on the opposite side. By the time we've reached the far end, the net is all back in the water and is full of salmon again. Then we reverse and repeat the picking process.

When the run is not as heavy, we pick the net from one end to the other, then drive the skiff to another net and pick it from one end to the other, then go back to the first net and repeat the process. Fish picking is a never-ending job.

Once the boat gets so full of fish it can't safely hold anymore, we go to shore. The people on shore back pickup trucks down to the edge of the beach, and we all pitch fish into the back of the trucks by hand for the trip to Cook Inlet Processors, the local processing plant.

Set-netters fish with a vengeance. When the fish are in, it's an around-the-clock job. We fish every legal tide. The nets stay in the water for every legal second. We're picking nets as long as there are fish. Sleep is rare — an hour here, two hours there. We get used to sleeping with the smell of Bag Balm on our hands, the feel of soggy socks in our leaky waders, the presence of salt crystals on our glasses and in our hair.

Only the most violent seas keep us on shore when there are fish to be picked. We expect to be pounded by waves and to return to camp drenched. During the few good, warm days, we can fish in T-shirts. As the summer ebbs and the light fades, we use headlamps at night.

Set-net fishermen in Cook Inlet are allowed three nets per permit. We had two permits, and thus were allowed six nets. We were fishing with five nets in the water, so we were getting ready to put in an outside set to give us our legal sixth net. An outside set is a net with both ends anchored away from the beach (as compared with an inside set, which has one end anchored at the beach). Our job that day was to set the anchors that would hold the net in place against the tremendous force of the tides.

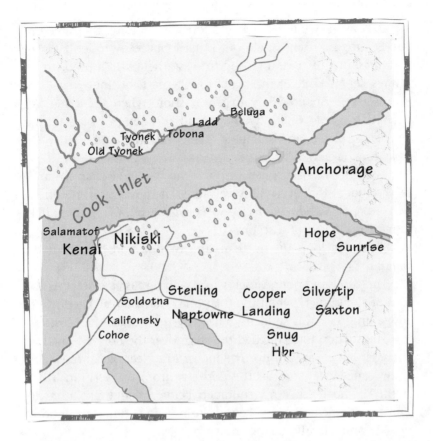

WE WENT THROUGH quite a procedure to create an anchor and get it out to the anchor site. At extreme low tide, I had used a bulldozer to push a thousand-pound boulder down to the shoreline. There I rigged it as an anchor, drilling it and attaching eye bolts. To the eye bolts I fastened a cable line, float line, floats, and buoys. Then we waited for high tide.

As the tide came in, the boulder disappeared beneath the water. The floats marked its location. At high tide, with the boulder now well beneath the surface, Lance and I pulled up to the floats in a twelve-foot aluminum skiff with a special hole in the center and a hand winch. Using the winch, we raised the sunken rock up off the bottom. Then we motored out toward the spot in deep water where we would lower the rock into place as an anchor.

Lance brought the float line around the side of the boat. We made a loop and placed it through a handle on the side in the bow of the boat. My job was to take care of the float line while sitting in the bottom of the bow. The float line would then keep the rock from swinging back and forth and fouling the cable line it was hanging from. I held onto that loop, ready to let it go the instant something went wrong. In case there was a problem we always kept a knife at the ready to cut the float line.

We were about 400 yards from shore when the cable line snapped. Instead of individual strands breaking one at a time, the whole cable line snapped! There was no time to cut the float line.

The float line screamed through the handle. For an instant I felt confident that everything was fine. There was a feeling of, *Ah, well, too bad we lost the rock, but everything is OK.* That thought lasted for a tenth of a second.

Then the loop in the float line twisted and bound in the handle.

The thousand-pound rock was dropping fast toward the bottom of Cook Inlet. When the float line bound up, all the force of the falling rock was suddenly taken by the side of the bow.

The sudden force pitched the stern over the bow. I leaped for the side. The stern shot up. The motor rose clear out of the water. I saw Lance catapulted to the port side from his position in the stern. The boat struck my shoulders before I could take a breath. The boat cupped over me like the closing of a coffin. It went down quickly and silently, taking me with it.

The torpedo-like speed forced water into my nose, under my eyelids, and into my mouth. The saltwater burned my nose. I swallowed some water to keep from choking. My hands groped helplessly in the darkening gray water.

The rock plummeted toward the ocean floor with the boat in tow and me trapped inside. The pain was excruciating in my head, in my eyes, and in my ears, which popped three times like warning shots.

I HAD ENDURED near-drowning experiences before. Shortly before my mother died six weeks earlier, we had talked about the time I almost drowned in the Mediterranean Sea, along the beach in Algiers. It is my very earliest memory; I was only one and a half years old. My memory was of a sensation that was very, very peaceful. I remember being underwater and feeling totally safe and totally calm before I was fished out by a stranger. Mom was the one who was having the panic.

As an adult, I came close to drowning while whitewater raft-ing and kayaking. What I learned from my experiences and those of close friends is that the faster you can get under control and relax, the sooner things are going to go right for you. You don't have control over everything. But you have to take your best shot, do it carefully, and avoid burning yourself out. You have to ad-just to the situation as quickly as you can. If you take too long to adjust, you *will* die.

SUDDENLY THE BOAT stopped. I stopped. I gained some resolve. I told myself, *Get centered quickly, Jimmy, or you won't have time to deal with this.*

The boat was suspended above me, bow down. Its built-in flotation tanks kept it from dropping completely to the seafloor as the huge boulder held it under. The contents spilled from the boat, and I became entangled in cable-laid rope. I groped in the dark, feeling the ropes, feeling the pressure build in my lungs.

I heard muffled metallic banging. More frightening, I remem-ber my own sounds of *uummp, uummp, uummp* as I tried to hold my breath and keep things under control. I grabbed the rim of the boat and struggled to clear myself from beneath it, but I was caught up in polypropylene line. The float line was wrapped around my leg.

I was vertical in the water, stranded midway between the bottom and the surface, thirty feet from life-giving oxygen. My chest waders were completely full of ice-cold water. My lungs pounded with every motion.

I had to find my Spyderco knife — the stainless steel knife favored by commercial fishermen for its razor-sharp serrated edge. I groped for the knife and felt it on its loop tied to my chest waders.

I opened the knife with one hand and sawed through the two loops of cable-laid rope that bound my leg, trying to avoid carving myself at the same time. Free of the rope, I shinnied out from under the boat. Here the light was better and I could see.

I looked up and saw the silver sheen of the surface. It seemed a long way. Some bubbles seemed to mock me as they rose easily upward. I kept my eyes fixed on the surface, with my head tilted back. I never looked back at the boat.

I felt a great sense of mental release, but the pressure on my lungs to breathe and the pounding in my chest convulsed my body. It made my eyes bulge and hurt.

I had at least thirty feet to swim before I could get air. Although my strength was dissolving, I decided there was no way in hell I was going to die there. Trying to calm myself, I started to swim carefully upward. My legs were heavy and barely moved as I reached for the surface.

Everything seemed in slow motion. I felt like I was swimming in Jell-O. The trip up seemed to last forever. I refused to quit, to accept death. I struggled upward, thrashing my arms and legs. I just kept swimming.

The thick waders produced incredible drag as I pulled them and all their trapped water. Now *I* was the Jell-O, trapped in neoprene. I had to deliberately shut off thoughts of oxygen.

I started to let air out when I was still about five or six feet under the water. I exhaled as much as I possibly could as I neared the surface. I remember seeing yellow and black dots, followed by a sort of darkening gray around me. I broke the surface and gulped air, coughing and choking and clearing my nose of saltwater. It had seemed to take hours to get there, although it was probably just a minute.

AS I BROKE the surface, I was seconds from death. All I could do was gasp, wondering if I could float and wondering where the land was.

I looked around and saw some buoys, which were about three feet in diameter. *I can reach the buoys,* I told myself. But the wind, which had been blowing about twenty miles an hour, had picked up and was blowing the buoys away.

I tried to relax to conserve energy and to regain some strength. I figured if I floated, my anxiety would go down ten points. I relaxed and was able to keep my head just above water.

I thought about something my dear mother had said just before she died: "You can do whatever you make up your mind you want to do."

I spotted Lance thirty feet away. He had no flotation at all, and he was having trouble. He had to take his hip waders and rain gear off in order to swim effectively. In the process of shedding his gear, he disappeared from sight a couple of times. Each time I wondered if he would come up again.

We swam toward each other, each very concerned about how the other was doing. Lance had been worried when I hadn't surfaced right after the boat went down. When he finally saw me, he yelled words of encouragement. He said we should try to swim for the buoys.

That didn't work out and burned up a lot of energy. Just then I spotted a small float thirty feet away, floating free and unaffected by the breeze. I kick-floated to it and managed to stuff it into my chest waders. I was now securely buoyant. I told Lance to come on over and we'd swim in together.

He said it would be better if he just swam for the shore, but he was concerned about leaving me. I told him not to worry: "Get going or you'll get tied up and then we're going to be in a world of hurt." He was a big, strong man who used to swim these cold waters for the fun of it when he was a kid.

We discussed the best action. I told him I felt that because he had no flotation of his own and because the water was so cold (forty degrees), he should head for shore. Swimming would help him maintain some body heat. Lance felt he could make it to shore, or at least to the outside buoy of the beach sets. I told him I would be fine. He started toward the beach.

I started angling toward the beach with the tide, paddling slowly, still trying to save energy. As long as I could float, I would be okay. I didn't want to use up any more energy because I didn't know how long I'd be in the water before shock crept over my body.

THE PEOPLE on the beach had seen our accident. Isam Hillary, an old salt who has fished out there for years and years with his sons, rushed over to the Hughes' fish site to report the accident. Lance's wife, Michelle, was there, with their two-year-old daughter, Cortney, and Lance's mother, Ina.

As Michelle and Ina looked out onto the water, they could see only one figure. They knew that one of us was below the surface with the boat, and they were terrified.

Chuck Nygard, a fellow teacher at my school who was also on our fishing crew, ran to our twenty-foot aluminum picking skiff and got it into the water. He and Ina jumped into the skiff and started for us.

They pulled up beside me and wrestled me aboard. Twenty minutes had elapsed since Lance and I had been tossed into the water. I didn't feel real cold, but I could hardly move. There was so much water in my waders that I couldn't sit or stand.

I lay down and stuck my feet in the air to empty the water out of the waders. I felt like a walrus in the bottom of the boat. Lying there, I started getting very cold, very quickly.

Meanwhile, Lance had managed to swim to the outside buoy a hundred feet from shore. We headed for him and picked him up.

In a short time we were safe on shore. I was shivering uncontrollably and headed straight into the *banya*, a little room like a sauna, with a fifty-five-gallon wood-fired barrel stove. Water is hosed onto the hot stove to generate steam.

As I sat there amid the steam, I could feel the banya driving the cold from my body like a shaman driving out an evil spirit. This little room that we used for getting clean on the beach turned out to be the great force that drove the symptoms of hypothermia away. My intense shivering slowed down and finally stopped.

Lance refused to go into the banya until he could go out and see our boat. He got a ride with his neighbors, but there was no boat to be seen. They retrieved some boards and the winch, which were still floating on the surface. Then they returned to shore to wait for low tide when they might be able to see the sunken boat.

Lance joined me in the banya, and we talked about what had happened. We only briefly acknowledged the fact that one or both of us could easily have been killed.

Lance wanted to retrieve the boat, even though we knew it would probably be swept away by the tide. At low tide, we got together with Lance's neighbors, the Hillarys, and motored out to the sunken boat in two other boats.

We looked and looked. Every once in a while the stern would show up and then disappear, like a ghost ship. The boat was floating underwater, tethered about forty feet from the bottom, suspended on the float line. Just like a bobber, only underwater.

It was a strange feeling to be back near the boat that nearly took me to my death. The boat was still threatening anyone who tried to get on it or near it.

As the tide receded, we were able to reach the float line with a knife taped to an oar. We cut the float line, freeing the boat from the anchor. The flotation tanks in the boat caused it to rise to the surface. We reached over the sides of our boats and bailed water from the newly emerged boat.

One of the helpers got into the boat and started bailing, but the boat started to sink again. He hung onto one of the other boats and escaped. The boat was still playing that phantom ship kind of thing. We finally got it fully afloat and towed it back to the beach.

My adventure was a good reminder of how frail we all really are. Nothing can totally prepare you for being faced with how rapidly circumstances can change. But when disaster hit, I was able to put my priorities in line. I got rid of a lot of the bull real fast and was able to focus on what matters and what doesn't. ■

THE END

Select Bibliography

Personal interviews
Anonymous. July 31, 1991. Anchorage.
Aronow, Jim. February 10, 1991. Anchorage.
Broussard, Ken. January 28, 1991. Anchorage.
Harbaugh, Mike. March 12, 1991. Wasilla, Alaska.
Kommer, Russell. April 9, 1991. Anchorage.
Mahay, Steve. May 8, 1991. Anchorage.
Misner, Darrel. March 12, 1991. Anchorage.

Written statements
Blackwell, Sonie. March, 1993. Juneau.
Dahle, Clyde. March 31, 1993. Anchorage.
Hewkin, Mark. January, 1991. Zion, Illinois.
Hundley, Amelia. April, 1991. Jacksonville, Florida.
Smith, Kevin. Summer, 1989. Douglas, Alaska.

Books
Burford, Virgil (as told to Walt Morey). *North to Danger*. New York: The John Day Company, 1950.
Oliver, Simeon. *Son of the Smokey Sea*. New York: Julian Messner, Inc. 1941.
Samson, Jack (Edited by). *Man and Bear*. "Brown Bear the Hard Way." Bob Brister. Clinton, New Jersey: The Amwell Press, 1979.

Periodicals
———. *Accidents in North American Mountaineering*. "Fall on ice, avalanches, no radio." Vol. 6, Number 1, issue 43. 20–24. New York: The American Alpine Club. 1990.
Elmore, Henry (as told to Larry Meyers). "The Salty Darkness and Sweet Victory." *The Alaska Sportsman*. 12–17, 29–30. May 1953.
Freedman, Lew. "Two Climbers Survive Week of Hell on Mountain." *Anchorage Daily News*. A1, A8–10. April 30, 1989.
Kelly, Sheldon. *Reader's Digest*. 93–99. October 1991.
Kreutzer, Vi Swanson. "Trapped in an Eighty-foot Tidal Wave." *Alaska Magazine*. 18–20. September 1980.
O'Donnell, Pat (as told to Jim Rearden). "Lost in the Talkeetnas." *The Alaska Sportsman*. 6–9, 28–30. August 1956.
Richard, Terry. "Tourists can hire pilot for flightseeing of Alaska Range." E 5. *The Oregonian*. March 11, 1993.

About the Author

Larry Kaniut and his wife, Pamela, came to Alaska in 1966 and never left. The premier collector of Alaskan adventure tales taught and coached for twenty-six years at A. J. Dimond High School in Anchorage before taking up writing full time. He is the author of the best-selling *Alaska Bear Tales* and *More Alaska Bear Tales*.

Larry Kaniut

Kaniut was born in Deer Park, Washington, in 1942, and spent a good deal of his first eighteen years getting to know the magnificent outdoor country between Washington's Cascade Mountains and the Snake River. He earned a master's degree in education before going to work at Dimond, where he taught English and reading and coached wrestling, football, track, and cross-country running.

Larry and Pamela raised two daughters, Ginger and Jill, and a son, Ben, teaching them a love for the great Alaska outdoors. Kaniut also had time to do some commercial fishing and to work on construction projects. He has long been active in teaching Sunday School at his church.

Larry and Pamela live in the home they built in 1970 on the outskirts of Anchorage.

If you enjoyed *CHEATING DEATH*, you will enjoy one of Larry Kaniut's other popular books:

ALASKA BEAR TALES. 318 pages, soft-bound, 5 3/8 by 8 3/8 inches. $12.95 U.S., $15.95 Canadian. ISBN 0-88240-232-3.

This is perhaps Alaska's all-time bestseller with more than 100,000 copies sold!

Nothing prepares you for a bear encounter better than learning from those who have experienced bears firsthand. *Alaska Bear Tales* is a collection of more than 200 real-life accounts filled with all the horror, courage, and even humor inherent when man meets bear.

MORE ALASKA BEAR TALES. 295 pages, soft-bound, 5 3/8 by 8 3/8 inches. $12.95, $15.95 Canadian. ISBN 0-88240-372-9.

In this sequel, Larry Kaniut takes us from the farthest reaches of the Alaska wilderness, right around the corner to familiar urban settings where man and bear face off with unpredictable outcomes.

To order these books, send $12.95 each (Washington residents add $1.06 state sales tax) plus $5 postage/handling for one book, $2 postage/handling for each additional book, to:

Epicenter Press
Fairbanks/Seattle

Box 82368
Kenmore Station
Seattle, WA 98028

ALASKA BEAR TALES and *MORE ALASKA BEAR TALES* are published by Alaska Northwest Books™, an imprint of Graphic Arts Center Publishing Co. of Portland, Oregon. Booksellers: Retail discounts are available by contacting Graphic Arts Center Publishing, 800-452-3032.

613.67 K132c
5/97
Kaniut, Larry.

Cheating death

ALBANY COUNTY
PUBLIC LIBRARY
LARAMIE, WYOMING

DEMCO